FIRE READY!

FIRE READY!

by Eric Dean

Western Skies Publishing
Albuquerque, New Mexico

Published by: Western Skies Publishing
                 P.O. Box 3793
                 Albuquerque, New Mexico 87190

Printed in the United States

Library of Congress Catalog Card Number: 95-60078

ISBN 0-9644945-5-8

Printed on recycled paper

To family and friends,
especially Mom, Dad, Sue,
Randy, and Crista.

Contents

Haystack Fire

Division A

WHEN I went to sleep on June 17th, I had no idea that something exciting was about to happen. The Fire Situation Report we got that day showed an increase in fire activity throughout New Mexico, the result of lightning strikes on the 14th and the 15th. There was no mention that many crews were being called out to fight the fires.

Our call-out came at 15 minutes after midnight on the 18th. Oscar, a supervisor, ran over to our cluster of houses and banged on Jerry's door six or seven times, loud and hard. The only time there is a knock on a firefighter's door in the middle of the night is when he's going somewhere. Sure enough, Jerry opened the door and Oscar asked, "You want to go on a fire?"

Jerry croaked out a "Yeah, sure." Then Oscar jogged over to my place.

I knew what was coming next, and had known from that first knock on Jerry's door. For the past three years, fire had been my life. Nervous and wide awake, I met Oscar at the door. He didn't need to knock.

"We want you and Jerry to go on a fire on the Gila National Forest," he said. "Feel like going? Are you ready to go?"

"Sure. I'm ready."

Oscar went back to his house to get some sleep. I stood alone in the kitchen, my whole body tingling with excitement. I quickly ate a small bowl of cold cereal, not knowing when the next meal would be.

Carrying my gear outside, I met Jerry, my good buddy. Jerry was from California, dark haired, deeply tanned, about my height but of a stockier build. He woke up early every morning and welcomed the sunrise with a leisurely cup of tea, even on his days off. He wouldn't have the chance today.

Jerry and I, wearing fire-resistant, forest-green pants and bumblebee-yellow shirts, checked over our gear. I tossed a couple pairs of fresh underwear and socks into my red pack. This call-out was just like all the rest. Get up in the middle of the night, stand around. Hurry up and wait.

It was a beautiful night. Orion and the Big Dipper were up there right where they should be at one o'clock in the morning. I savored the coolness. In a matter of hours we would be sweating on the fireline.

The chief ranger came by in his truck and picked us up. We joined the others at the fire cache and rounded up cases of fusees (pronounced "fyu-zee", they resemble highway flares), MRE military rations, water canteens, plus bundles of pulaskis and shovels, and loaded them in the truck we would be driving to the Gila. Then we waited for the rest of the crew to arrive from the other park.

Jerry and I leaned back on our field packs, trying to get some rest. There would be little of that precious commodity for the next several days. Energy conservation is the secret to firefighting, because on the fireline you go into energy debt. In other words, enjoy the good times while you can. Sometimes it's fun being lazy, especially when you know what's coming next.

The others showed up in their trucks, and we were on our way to Silver City, New Mexico. Our driver claimed he wasn't tired so the rest of us zonked out in the back for the four-hour drive. We had an uneventful breakfast at a cafe in Silver City. The waitresses were really cute. As soon as a guy is sent out on a fire dispatch, all women immediately gain several points on the Beauty Scale.

We finally arrived at the staging area, where the crews were organized. Somebody with a clipboard came by and asked each of us for our weight, then wrote the figures down. This was good, very good news — it meant they were thinking about helicoptering us into the fire.

We could see the fire. Burning about six miles to the east, in mixed pine trees and brush in very steep terrain, it wasn't doing much at all. It sent up several thin, grey towers of smoke, and, as someone remarked, it looked like a real bitch to put out. It had already burned about 400 acres, a holdover fire from the lightning three days before.

No dice on the helicopter ride. Darn! We hung around for another hour, four crews with twenty people each. Everybody seemed cool and collected, joking around, sleeping, playing cards, oiling their boots. Firefighters are really good at acting casual, even when deep down there is a churning little voice saying, "I wonder what's going to happen next?" Whatever does happen next is usually the decision of someone you'll probably never meet, someone in a command post or logistics center somewhere, calling for crews. Your crew is available, so you go. It's weird knowing that some stranger, with unknown motives and plans, is calling your name and controlling your destiny. There is a strange, unnerving sense of security — if that's what freedom from responsibility is — as someone else calls the shots that could change your life.

"What's the name of the fire, anyway?" I asked somebody in Overhead, the command team.

"Haystack. That's Haystack Mountain, where it's burning. What's the name of your crew?"

"Sonora."

Maybe I shouldn't have said anything. A few minutes later he hollered, "Sonora!" and we got back into the vehicles.

A couple of miles down the main road we turned onto a dirt road and headed east for three or four more miles, the driver not even slowing down for the cattle guards. Some folks rolled up the windows to keep the dust out, even though pretty soon we'd be wallowing in dirt on the fireline so it really didn't matter. We pulled up near a muddy stock tank, unloaded, and our crew boss, Henry, hurried away to the command post tent to get more instructions.

The rest of us lounged under some juniper trees, 19 people crammed into the shade. Firefighters are miracle workers when it comes to creating luxury out of nothing. Entire crews will disappear into the shade of a single tree during rare break times, only to emerge with wishful thinking after the break is over.

We ate MRE's for dinner. It was 3:30 in the afternoon. We guzzled water from one-gallon canteens, stretched out on the dirt, and slept in the shade. Life was good.

"Dammit! Ants! There are ants all over the place!" We popped up, looked around hurriedly, brushed off a few strays, tucked our pantcuffs in our socks, and went back to sleep. At least then they couldn't crawl up our legs. I had been using my field pack for a pillow, but the headlamp inside kept poking me in the neck, so I moved my head off the pack onto something really soft and comfortable. Much better! When I woke up, I found out it was a dried cowpie. By then it really didn't matter.

Henry came back to tell us we had our line assignment and would be moving out. We ambled over to the trucks, snatching occasional glances at the fire to the north.

The road was steep as we edged into the foothills. We got our first sweet sniff of wood smoke. It smells really good, in moderation, at least. The road got even steeper. The truck lost traction, so we piled out and gave it a push. The driver gave it too much gas, and showered us with sand and gravel.

About ten minutes later, the smoke grew thicker,

bitter, and we could see it blowing in the windows. My heart started beating faster. We had to blink more, and somebody sneezed. I looked over at Jerry. He looked across at me and smiled. The truck lurched over a big rock and I bumped against the fellow beside me. It felt good to know that I wasn't in this alone.

Division B

THE ROAD dead-ended and we all got out. We gathered into squads and chose whichever tools our squad boss told us to get. I grabbed a pulaski and hustled to get my gear on. You could hear the sharp plastic "click!" of the buckles snapping shut as we put on our packs.

My pack contained the following things:

Fire shelter

6 quarts of water

Headlamp with extra "D" batteries

Compass

Emergency space blanket

4 sheets of writing paper

2 pens

Roll of orange flagging

Small bottle of insect repellent

Extra pair of leather fire-resistant gloves

Camera

Chicken a la King MRE

4 granola bars

2 cans of juice (1 tomato, 1 orange)

4 fusees ("fyu-zee" flares)

Windbreaker

Wool shirt

Red Card (I was squad boss certified.)

Poncho

Sack lunch

Pocket first aid kit

10' parachute cord

Pocket knife

Whistle

4 mini-wedges (to tighten pulaski handles)

Extra boot lace

Spare pair of prescription glasses

At the beginning of a shift, with full canteens, our packs would weigh in at 30 pounds.

The last of the trucks pulled in. The driver turned

off the engine. Another seven or eight people climbed out, a tailgate thunked shut, and everything became strangely quiet. It always did, before the chain saws fired up and the hand-tools started thrashing the brush and clanging off the rocks. On this fire, Overhead wanted all branches and brush cleared in a six-foot wide firebreak, with a three-foot wide fireline of bare dirt running right down the middle. All the trees, brush, roots, pine needles, grasses, etc. had to go. This was a standard fireline. Most of the dirty work would be done with the hand-tools.

A person quickly loses his individual identity and becomes known by the tool he or she is using, a "Pulaski" or a "Shovel." Someone calling for help does not ask for people, he yells for tools. "Hey, I need four Pulaskis and a couple of Shovels up here on the double!"

I prefer being a Shovel.

Working our way downhill, not even a quarter mile from the parking area, our crew took the lead. We were cutting awesome fireline and feeling good. Our fire shirts were stained with sweat, covered with dirt, and our field packs had settled nicely on our backs. We had lightened our load by several pounds, having drunk a warm quart of water in the two hours since we started. My glasses were covered with sweat, dust, and mud where the two mixed. It felt good to work hard.

We followed pink strips of flagging that Henry had tied to branches as he located the easiest route for the fireline. He led the way. The crew boss always does. Henry really knew how to hustle, too. He saved the rest of us a lot of work by finding the easiest way, avoiding thick stands of trees and brush. When you see your boss working hard for you, well, you tend to try your darndest to make him look good. He then sees how hard his crew is working, and works even harder to make your job easier. "You rub my back, I'll rub yours." It works.

Hours later, at dusk we got to the bottom of the hill, where Sacaton Creek was doing its best to imitate a burbling brook. Better luck next time, creek. The creek bottom was empty of trees and brush; wide, rocky, and wet. Since this made the ultimate fireline, we gave our tools a rest and followed it upstream. The only problem was that, being around eight o'clock in the evening, it was getting dark. And nothing is more precarious than walking on wet rocks, wearing heavy boots, and carrying a pack and a tool — with only a headlamp for light.

We walked single file, twenty of us heading

upstream in the tail-end of the twilight, the sound of shuffling feet broken by frequent "clunks" as someone stubbed a toe on a rock, followed by two or three short, rapid, skidding steps as he recovered his balance. Now and then a "clank" (pulaski) or a "clink!-ding ding ding" (shovel) was heard, followed by a loud "crunch" as the owner of the tool sprawled on the rocks. Next came a "splash!" if he or she was near the water. Either way, "Son of a bitch!" and then "Hey, are you okay?" Oh yeah, somewhere in there is a "chink" when the hard hat falls off, and sometimes even a melodic "crash!..tinkle-tinkle" as the headlamp lens shatters into a hundred pieces. So here's what a fall sounds like:

"Clunk, shuffle-shuffle, clank/clink!-ding-ding-ding, crunch, splash!, chink, crash!..tinkle-tinkle, Son of a bitch! Hey, are you okay?"

It was 10 p.m. We'd left the creek and were chopping fireline through a shortcut. Awake since midnight — almost 22 hours — we were getting tired. The hand-tools didn't chop where we wanted them. They were so dull by now that it really didn't matter anyway. The shovels kept stubbing on hidden rocks and roots, burying into soft-looking piles of pine needles or duff and smashing point-first into hidden rocks that went down to the very center of the earth.

Strange things begin to happen to a crew when its really tired. Almost everybody goes at half speed, and those who aren't soon will be. There's always one wise guy who still has some get-up-and-go, though. But that's okay, because pretty soon he'll run out of gas, only to have his place taken over by someone else who gets his twentieth second wind of the shift.

It happens to all of us. When we're feeling good: "Gee, I'm not tired after all! This is great!" while ripping into a log with a shovel, or slashing through two-inch thick saplings in a single swipe. Ten minutes later, that luscious feeling fades, and is replaced by sinking reality. "I'm wiped out. Why did I waste all my precious energy on that stupid log? Now, how am I going to lift my feet over this rock? Can I make it to the end of the shift?"

Henry saw what was happening to the crew. It's like watching — in living color — images from a horror zombie movie, only everybody is wearing matching yellow long-sleeved shirts and forest-green pants, swinging tools and sweeping headlamps. Henry gathered everybody around and told us to get some sleep.

We were twenty feet from Sacaton Creek, smack dab at the bottom of a large, rocky gully. It was cold.

We could see our breath. The chilled, moist, midnight air lazily wafted around our sweat-soaked, steaming bodies.

It didn't take a lot of persuasion for us to take off our packs. We scattered, each hoping to find a level area big enough to stretch out. I was lucky, and found a nice, cozy spot which the others had somehow overlooked. Then I found out, by the fading light of my headlamp, that my little plot of paradise was a literal garden of poison ivy. Luckily, I didn't have much of a reaction, and the ferocious itching down the middle of my back went away after a couple of days.

I opened my pack and took out my wool shirt, windbreaker, and space blanket, the latter saved for an emergency. This qualified. With the cold, damp mountain air settling around my exhausted body, and daylight still five frigid hours away . . . yes, this was definitely an emergency. On went the windbreaker and out came the space blanket, the plastic crinkling like a crisp cellophane wrapper. It was ultra-light — so thin you could see through it — and covered with a shiny layer of aluminum, which, in theory, reflects back your body heat. Ha!

A friend of mine had to use one in a similar setting and told me that the secret is to first tuck it around your knees, then work your way up to your hips, ribs, shoulders, and finally tuck it around your head, leaving a little air gap somewhere around your armpit so you don't suffocate. I piled up a thick layer of pine needles and poison ivy leaves, lay back on top of that, and used the emergency blanket as recommended. It must have been designed for circus dwarfs. It was way too short! Knees and below were left exposed to the elements. It was a disaster.

Every breath I took was cut short by the plastic being sucked into my mouth, making a dull pop as it stretched tight between my lips. Condensation drops began to drip down onto my face. Hmm. I solved both dilemmas by breathing through my nose, and could breathe deeply without fear of suffering a hernia. It really is amazing how much water is given off when you breathe out through your mouth, much more so than when breathing through your nose.

Before I tucked myself in, I had looked up and seen the constellation Orion, in the same place it had been the day before at one o'clock in the morning, as it drifted through the frozen chasm of space — an unwelcome thought when one is on the verge of freezing in the middle of a rocky drainage in southern New Mexico. Exactly twenty-four hours earlier, I had been roused from a warm, relaxed slumber, never having heard of a place called Sacaton Creek.

I wish I could say that I soon dozed off into restful sleep, but that just wasn't the case. As the expression goes: It's always darkest just before it turns pitch black. How true!

Amid the crinkling of the space blanket, I could hear people on the crew tossing and turning in their plastic ponchos and emergency blankets, shivering, trying unsuccessfully to get comfortable and warm. Somebody blurted out, "Damn, it's cold!" which did little to help matters. To make things even worse, we went "off the clock" — we stopped being paid — at midnight, meaning that this suffering was coming out of our own pockets. To be miserable when you're being paid is bad enough; to do it for free is really the pits.

I might have slept several consecutive minutes but I'm not really sure. Call it more of an out-of-body experience. What is certain is that after an eternity I began to hear voices, and an occasional forced chuckle mixed in with the conversation. I lifted an edge of the blanket and peeked out. There, bless their souls, were several of my companions huddled around a small campfire. The cheerful snapping and popping beckoned to me. I stumbled over to them, clutching my emergency blanket, found some pieces of wood, and added them to the collection of firewood. Then I leaned back against a log. Staring into the fire, feeling the warmth oozing into my body — it felt so good — I slumped over on my side, and soon was fast asleep.

It lasted 30 glorious minutes. All too soon, I was surrounded by deep, groaning voices, the universal sound of protest, the sound of people being woken up in the dark and told they were moving out. It was 3 a.m. I could barely keep my eyes open.

Someone offered me a small slab of dehydrated hashed brown potatoes from an MRE, which I accepted and ate, not knowing any better. Then we put on our packs, picked up our tools, and took our places in line by squads, single file. It was the same formation as three hours before. Only now we were heading down Sacaton Creek, back to fire camp.

We marched solemnly, stumbling over unseen branches and rocks, the once-white light from our headlamps now a tired, lazy amber and getting weaker. The first signs of dawn began to show themselves; the stars faded and disappeared altogether. Hesitant rays of sunshine streamed over the horizon. Daylight does amazing things to a person's spirit, and soon we were all walking with a genuine spring in our steps.

We left Sacaton Creek, slowly climbed up the hill,

following our fireline completed the afternoon before. Being in squad one, the squad at the front, I rarely got to see the finished fireline, and it really looked great. This was our work. We had done this.

The hill seemed to go on forever, and with the morning sun warming things up I began to break a sweat. We walked over the crest of a low ridge. Below us was a small cluster of pea-green Forest Service trucks, waiting to take us back to camp. One of the drivers, chuckling, said, "I'll bet you folks had a cold night last night." Jerk.

Division C

Fire camp; home sweet home. We climbed out of the trucks. All of our gear was right where we had left it, in a big heap in the back of another truck. We unloading our red packs, selecting a suitable site to sleep 20 people. Those of us who had brought tents put them up, just in case it rained, which by definition it almost never does when you're on a forest fire.

Fire camp had become a bustling place in our absence, with a command trailer, first aid tent, tented dining area, and half a dozen port-a-potties. There were now eight crews in camp, most of them from California or New Mexico. The famed Redding Hot Shots, one of the premier fire crews in the nation, were there, walking everywhere single file as a crew,

wearing matching tee-shirts and being very profession-
al. Some of their discipline must have rubbed off on
us; when word got out that they were serving hot
breakfasts we lined up single file and walked over for
some chow. We had never lined up to eat before, but
all the other crews were doing it now and we did not
want to look like bozos.

It was now 10 o'clock and the day was still warming up. Breakfast was scrambled eggs, hash browns,
sausage or ham — your choice — plus bread, juice,
and milk. All fire camp breakfasts are pretty much the
same.

These caterers live an interesting life. Each summer
they travel all over the West with semi-tractor trailers
filled with walk-in freezers, stoves, cooking gear, and
enough frozen, canned, and fresh food to feed several
hundred firefighters for several days. When that runs
out they go into town and buy out the local supermar-
ket. Cooks and servers travel along. They always pitch
their tents right beside the trailers. Sometimes they'll
set them up under the trailers if the weather looks bad.
On a big fire they sleep in shifts, 12 hours on and 12
hours off, taking turns cooking, serving, or preparing
hundreds and hundreds of sack lunches. It's activity
around the clock! The food is usually really good, too:
steak or chicken, salad, potatoes, canned vegetables,

canned peaches with cottage cheese, and Hostess fruit pies for dessert make up a typical dinner, all-you-can-eat. Any time day or night, you can walk over and get a hot meal. Nothing is better for morale than knowing that after a long, tough shift on the fireline at least you'll be eating well when you get back to camp.

After breakfast, we straggled back in small groups to our little encampment, roped off now with limp strips of red flagging. Someone in Overhead had written our crew name on a piece of cardboard and stuck it in front, but it fell over.

Jerry and I set out to fill our canteens. We always did this before bedtime so we would be ready to leave when we woke up. On the way back we discovered a huge, converted water trough filled with ice-cold Gatorade, soda, and fruit. Nearby were several cases of granola bars. We snagged some, coming back heavily-laden and telling everybody about our find. A couple of guys hurried over before all the root beers were gone, thanking us as they walked by. Sharing helped create a close crew, and that made all the difference.

Off came my boots, on went the tennis shoes. After trudging around in heavy leather work boots for the whole shift the tennis shoes felt airy light — it's as if they might come flying out from underneath, taking me with them up into the sky. There's not much comfort in fire camp. You have to make the most with what you have.

Henry came back from a meeting with Overhead and said we were heading back out at 4:30 that afternoon. We had six hours to rest, and it was going to be another rough night. If you start the shift in mid-afternoon, then the earliest you'll be getting back is nine or ten o'clock the next morning. In other words, try to get some sleep! Every little bit helps. But it was going to be difficult. It was already 90 degrees and the flies were out en masse. I tried to sleep outside, but the bugs were bad so I crawled inside the tent. It was stifling hot and awful green inside, with no hint of a breeze, so back outside I went. Several guys on the crew were already snoring loudly. I envied them. I took some earplugs from my red pack and slept for almost three hours.

My red pack, designed to carry enough personal gear for two weeks, contained the following things:

3 tee-shirts
6 pairs of underwear
10 pair of socks (5 pair wool/ 5 pair liner socks)
Long underwear

Wool cap

Book (something funny)

2 toothbrushes (in case I lost one)

Toothpaste

Dental floss

Shampoo (doubles as laundry detergent)

Notebook

Wool gloves

Extra pair leather work boots

2 spare bandanas

Shorts (for swimming, or wearing around fire camp)

Tennis shoes

Extra pair fire pants

Extra fire shirt

Fully-outfitted red packs weigh about forty pounds. Everybody carries pretty much the same stuff. We were limited by space and weight — red packs couldn't weigh more than forty pounds — but even then some folks lived on the wild side and carried boot oil, a pocket radio, a hacky sack, or extra underwear.

I woke up, partially rested, groggy, and incredibly thirsty, drank a warm Gatorade and munched on some fruit and granola bars. It was almost time to eat dinner. A crew always eats a big meal before it goes out on the line. I changed back into my boots. Somebody from Overhead came by and dropped off a big box of batteries for our headlamps. I put some fresh ones in mine, knowing it was going to be a long, dark night. Henry, the crew boss, got everybody lined up and we ambled over for dinner. We usually only eat one serving before going out on the line. Anything to avoid having gas and belching while swinging a pulaski.

After dinner, Henry gave us our customary briefing. We were to be dropped off at the same spot as the afternoon before. Following our day-old fireline and then Sacaton Creek, we would branch off and head up a ridge to the north, finishing some handline that a crew had been working on during the day shift. It sounded good, and we were ready to go.

If we had known what was going to happen during this shift, we might not have been so eager.

Division D

OUR SACK lunches were piled high in a big card-board box, beside the batteries. I opened mine and looked inside. The usual: two ham sandwiches on white bread, a candy bar, a crushed bag of potato chips, a red apple, two sticks of gum, a small can of apple juice, salt, pepper, and little packets of mustard and mayonnaise, the kind you get at fast food restaurants. This was my first sack lunch of the fire season. I tried not to get too nostalgic as I stuffed it into my pack.

The truck ride to the same drop point was uneventful — the usual dust, bumps, and smoke, the struggling engine, and branches scraping the windows. The ride seemed to go quickly, and before we knew it we were walking and sliding — almost surfing — down the old fireline. Only seven hours had passed since we had struggled up that very trail, and despite several hours of sleep we were all dog tired.

It was hot. Rabbits hid in the shade, lizards ran for their lives. Dust swirled up from our boots. Once you started sneezing it was hard to stop. We stumbled over root stubs and rocks. They seemed to reach out and grab our boots.

We got to the creek and headed upstream. With little conversation, we arrived where the day shift had finished work. It had been an all-women Apache crew from Arizona, and they had done a really nice job. In the afternoon light, the fireline looked great. It was 12 feet wide and chopped free of all trees, branches, and grasses. Only short stubs remained where thick brush as tall as a person had been growing.

Alex, our sawyer, fired up his chain saw with a hard yank on the starter cord. The sawyer's job is to cut away the trees, heavy brush, and downed logs. He is assisted by someone known as a swamper. Depending on the conditions, there might even be two or three swampers. They pull away the freshly-cut branches and logs. They also watch out for the sawyer, keeping an eye out for unpredictable things like trees falling the wrong way, or branches crashing down from a tree being felled, or burning embers falling down the sawyer's back when he cuts a flaming tree. The list of bad things that can happen to a sawyer is endless. The risks become even more harrowing when the work is done at night, by the light of a headlamp, or the fire itself.

After the sawyer and swamper come the hard-working Pulaskis, four, five, or six people using the combination axe/hoe to chop brush left by the chain saw team and grub out the roots. Fire can follow shallow roots underground and cross the line unnoticed. Pulaskis define the fireline. Chop with the axe head and grub with the hoe. Don't work too close together — those pulaskis will bite! Watch out for your toes!

Next come the down-and-dirty Shovels, half a dozen of them. They take short, compact swipes at the ground, hunkered down so low they could play leapfrog if they wanted. Get that elbow braced against a knee for maximum leverage and swing with your hips; the sharp side edge of the tool does all the work, scraping away the debris churned up by the Pulaskis and pitching it outside the line, away from the fire. Keep that motion short and sweet. Try not to hit any rocks. Scrape...step...scrape...step. Repeat, endlessly.

At the end of the line will be a few McLeods, people using long-handled fire rakes. Interspersed among them will be more Pulaskis and Shovels. It's a good way to get the fireline really clean. All you want to see is dirt.

The ridge we were working was fairly steep, covered with jagged, softball-sized rocks which broke loose when we put full weight on them. Dangerous conditions to work in: a sharp tool or chain saw in your hands, 25-30 pounds of pack flopping around on your back. Rocks tipping over and rolling. It was getting dark.

We progressed slowly, and 200 yards later tied in with a thick rock outcropping. We didn't have to cut line, since there was nothing there to burn. Good news! We skipped that section, but it gave the impression that we'd cut more line than we actually had. Nobody complained.

By now, I was swamping for Alex, working close to the saw and grabbing the cut brush and branches, then throwing them outside the line. I liked watching the branches and limbs sail away downhill. My earplugs were working well; all sounds other than Alex calling to me or gunning the saw were blocked out. Without earplugs, the up-close sound of the saw slashing and tearing and shredding the brush was terrifying. Hours went by.

We saw flames for the first time.

By the looks of them, they had backed down the drainage to the northwest and were beginning to act up. Occasional flares of red fire could be seen torching off small clusters of trees. That was strange — it should not be doing that at 10 o'clock at night! Fires usually quiet down at night. And why was the wind acting squirrelly, changing directions on a whim? Why wasn't the higher nighttime humidity making the fire quiet down?

Oh, sure, our position was secure. Even if the fire were to suddenly reach the bottom of the drainage, cross sides, and make an upslope run at us, we still had two good options.

One. *Retreat at a high rate of speed down the fireline we'd just made and outflank the fire.*

Two. *Drop off the lee side of the ridge we were working. Fire usually travels so slowly downhill that we could easily get away.*

We kept working steadily, catching a quick look from time to time at the fire across the drainage, a steep, wooded valley half a mile wide, narrowing as it drained to the south. We could see its width by the flickering light of the fire. Somewhere down below was Sacaton Creek.

It was almost 11 o'clock and time for our second dinner of the day. We put down our tools and took out our sack lunches. One of the division bosses stopped by to chat just as we sat down. Large fires are divided into divisions, Division A, Division B, and so on. Each division boss is responsible for his portion of the fire. The division boss, a nice fellow, talked for a few moments with Henry about fire behavior in this part of the country.

Suddenly his radio squawked. We could all here the message, broadcast to a crew working way above us.

"Hey!, you have some fire cooking below you. Watch it!" Then we heard the distant whoosh of the flames as the fire made a small uphill run. The sky to the north turned hot red. A few minutes later we heard on the radio that the fire had hit the fireline and slopped over, creating several small spotfires across the line. This minor flareup would play a major part in our lives within several hours, but we didn't know it then. The fire across the drainage stood out in stark, flaming three-dimension, a skirmish line of small flames stretching along the slope across from us, still a third of a mile away.

All we could do was watch and eat our sack lunches. Jerry, sitting beside me, said, "I'm glad I'm not up there!" when the fire flared. I sat back against my pack, wearing a windbreaker to fight off the chill. It gets cold taking a break at night, when you're all sweaty. The sandwiches were good, and far off in the distance we could see the twinkling lights of a small town, probably in Arizona. Someone said he thought it was Morenci, but nobody knew for sure.

When we were down to the last of our potato chips, we were given our instructions. Our crew would continue up the ridge, then improve and widen the line that a previous crew had made farther ahead. Once that was done, we would follow the fireline back down to Sacaton Creek. The crews above us would burn out the line, working their way downhill along the top of the ridge. We picked up our tools and had at it. The work was easy, and soon we had covered a couple hundred yards.

But then the ridgeline got steep, too steep to walk straight up, and we had to traverse the slope in snug zig-zags. Occasionally, one of us near the front accidentally stepped on a lunchbox-sized rock and it broke loose, slowly skidding, then rolling, and finally bouncing in increasing arcs as it picked up speed.

"Rock! Rock!"

The people below would flash their headlamp beams uphill. There it is!, reaching out a hand or a tool to try to stop it. More often than not the attempt would fail, and the person would lose balance, sliding downhill, dropping their tool, and just that quickly there were three objects working together with gravity, a person, a tool, and the original rock, each tumbling the same way. Down. Sooner or later, they all came to rest.

"Hey, are you okay?"

"Yeah, dang! Son of a bitch!"

You hear that a lot on the fireline.

By now I was carrying the chain saw. We took turns with the hard jobs. With a shovel in my left hand, the saw over my right shoulder, a full pack on my back, breathing choking dust, losing my balance every few steps, and watching out for those rocks, well, I was definitely not having a good time. All you can think about is how incredibly tired and miserable you are, but then again, so is everybody else on the crew. It really is true; misery does like company.

We had stopped midway up the slope to catch our breath and get a drink when word traveled up from the back that two people on the crew were having a rough time. One was a poorly-conditioned woman whose husband was also on the crew, and the other was a heavy smoker who wanted fire experience to put on his resume. They just didn't realize what this was all about, the danger, the inherent seriousness of the whole business. This wasn't a game. So these two folks gave up.

It meant that those of us who continued on would have to look out for them, and, with their place in line vacant, work that much harder while they sat out. Not a good way to make friends.

Those of us in the front finally topped out and looked back downhill at the others. All we could see in the blackness were the headlamps weaving their way along the turns in the line. It was so steep it was like looking down a black elevator shaft with a dozen bright fireflies twinkling about.

One of the division bosses came by again. He said he was so pleased with our work that he was going to let us continue up the line and meet up with the other crews. Then, *we* were going to burn out as we went back down toward the creek, igniting the down-hill side of the line with our fusees and letting fire creep downhill, "burning out" the area between our line and the primary fire. When the two fires met, they would cancel each other out, and then all we had to do was mop-up along the perimeter. I wasn't unhappy to hear the news, even though it meant walking uphill another quarter mile or so. I loved burning out. Everybody does.

We followed his directions and soon came across several open areas on the top of the ridge. It was here that we left the two people who were too worn out to continue. Two crews that had been following us from Sacaton Creek arrived a few minutes later. They volunteered to remain there with our two folks while we hurried uphill and began burning out. We set out single file, following the fireline which by now cut through dense, almost continuous stands of pine and Douglas fir trees. The fireline no longer followed the top of the ridge; rather, it eased downhill on the side where the fire was burning below near the bottom of the drainage. Hmmm.

One thing I had learned about firefighting was that when things go bad, they really go bad. That lesson was about to be reinforced.

Division E

WE ARRIVED at a narrower handline running through heavy timber, with moderate brush mixed in. The fireline looked pretty wimpy, but this was what we had to burn out from, igniting a series of small, overlapping fires along the downhill, and then making sure the flames didn't jump over to the other side of the line and race uphill. Only Henry and Alex would be doing the actual burning.

I took Jerry's fusees from his pack, then he gave me mine. We looked down and across at the fire.

"Looks like a perfect prescribed burn to me," he said, "getting rid of the dead logs and brush. This place could use a good fire."

He walked down the line to meet up with his

squad. We were almost ready to burn.

The crew was going to flip-flop in its footsteps, with the last squad becoming the leaders and what had been the lead squad, mine, becoming the last. Alex and Henry would go to the front and ignite the burnout. We would follow behind and keep it under control. Henry gave me his radio, since Alex had one and they didn't need two. I was going to be the tail-end Charlie, the last man in the group, and would radio to them if the fire crossed over the line. The winds were perfect: gentle and downslope, but for some reason the air was still very dry, and was warmer than it should have been at one o'clock in the morning. The breeze felt good passing over my neck.

Henry gave us some last minute instructions and started down the line.

Suddenly the wind changed directions. A blast of dry wind blew hard in our faces. Far down below, beyond a hump in the hill that was blocking our view, a dull roar started up. Adreneline kicked in. At the same time, my radio blared.

"Sonora, you've got fire below! Get out of there!" Somebody was shouting into his radio — really excited. We paused for a split second, a stream of options flashing through our minds. Is it just a little flareup? Should we go back down the fireline? Should we follow it uphill? What should we do?

The fire decided for us.

Its roar increased, and a fuzzy red glow lit up the downhill, masked by the heavy trees that stood in front of us. The roar intensified by the second. Somebody yelled, **"Oh my God! Here it comes!"**

Suddenly the world changed, and everybody moved at once. Henry and Alex took off down the line to check on the folks left behind, both running so fast it was incredible. I couldn't help but think that I had never seen anybody run that fast before.

But that thought was overpowered by another: I could be dead in a minute. This fire could kill me. RUN!

I began running uphill, following the line, my legs driven by an instinct and emotion I had never felt so clearly. Fear. Some of my friends behind me were yelling, but the sounds made no sense. Their cries were drowned out by the shrieking roar of the fire. We ran. I looked over my left shoulder and saw the flames. Oh God! (A lookout on another crew later estimated the flames to be 200 feet tall.)

My face felt the heat of the flames. I turned away from the fire, concentrating on my footing. I didn't know where I was running, I was simply following the fireline and hoping that it went somewhere good. Way up ahead, somebody on another crew stopped in the middle of the line to take a picture of the flames. Not here! Not now!

"Move it! Move it!" I yelled. The words sounded desperate, almost hysterical, and it scared me that such sounds could come from my mouth. The fire intensified. The ground all around us was lit up like orange daylight. It was like high noon in the summer, it was that bright. The shadows were going the wrong way, uphill. The air got really hot, and as I ran I screamed to myself, "On no! Oh no!" over and over. I looked over my shoulder again and saw the rest of the crew strung out behind. Jerry was the guy at the very end, closest to the flames, and I felt desperately like yelling, "Run, Jerry! Run!" But I didn't.

We had been running through a small opening in the forest, but now we entered a thick stand of stunted pine trees, growing close together and making running difficult, catching our sleeves, poking our legs. Somehow we had left the fireline. There was no trail. We ran desperately through the trees, each of us finding our own route, headlamps flickering in the shadows. I ran frantically, knocking into small trees. I stumbled over a rock and dropped one of the shovels I had been carrying. I had been running with a shovel in each hand. Two shovels? Where had the other one come from?

I tripped again and nearly went down, and thought, with alarming clarity, "How stupid can you get! Tripping over a rock as you're about to get wiped out by a forest fire!"

We had been running for more than a minute. A minute is a long time. The whole downhill was on fire. Fire had cut us off in back and was trying to get in front of us. If it cut us off we wouldn't have a chance. Flames cast a dancing mosaic of strange patterns and colors onto the rocks. Fire. The only way I can describe it is ENERGY. It was energy in its purest form.

It wanted to kill us, all of us. I burst out of the trees and into a small clearing. When I had entered the thick stand I thought I would never make it out. All these thoughts — and so many others — flying through my mind like a laser beam bouncing off mirrors at crazy angles, without beginning or end. Everything seemed to be happening at once. If there is such a thing as Hell I really believe I know what it's like.

Then the fire seemed to change directions and move away from us, angling behind. I slowed down for a moment. Then, just as suddenly, it burst toward us, huge flames blasting into the night sky as trees which had been living peacefully for over a century exploded in flames and died. Looking at those huge trees quiver then erupt into liquid fire, I knew that we, people, were the lucky ones. At least we could try to flee. But how could I feel sorry for those trees as they burst into the very flames that threatened our lives? Somehow, I did. What a crazy thing the world had suddenly become.

I ran, frantic, absorbing all these thoughts and twisted emotions. The flames towered behind us. The back of my neck got hot enough to sting. To be a hundred yards from the fire and get a flash sunburn — even now I have difficulty believing it really happened. And how frustrating it was to be running so hard yet be making no progress against the flames. The fire was matching us, stride for stride. It was pacing itself. It was alive, and it wanted us. I know what it's like to be hunted.

Everything had become so crazy! I was yelling to myself, "I can't believe it, I can't believe it!" yet knew it was real. Confused, I ran, a stranger to these feelings and thoughts which had suddenly become a part of my life. Strange noises came from my mouth, plaintive whimpers begging for sympathy and understanding but getting none. One moment I was inside looking out, then outside looking in, and suddenly nothing I had believed in and lived for made any sense at all.

Drowning out everything else was the omnipotent,

drenching roar of the fire; pulsing, angry, dominant. The screeching hiss of a single tree consumed by flames, amplified by a thousand. Each tree, shrieking and howling in protest, powerless, sounding strangely like a huge bedsheet tearing violently in a savage wind, thousands making the screams of the Devil.

We ran.

And suddenly it was over.

Opening up in front of us was the most beautiful rockslide we had ever seen, waiting with open arms. We ran over the jagged rocks, tripping and stumbling in desperation, in appreciation. Rocks, in the past tumbling downhill into our ranks, now welcoming. Safety.

We hopped rock-to-rock high into the clearing, putting as much distance between us and the fire as possible. But it didn't feel like enough.

The fire shifted to the south and the east, and then it dawned on me why. While we were eating dinner — when that small run had taken place far above us — and Jerry had said "I'm glad I'm not up there!" — that's where we had just been. We had unknowingly run past the burned out area. The burned area offered nothing to the second, more intense, run, so the fire changed directions, seeking fuel for its appetite in another direction. That meant we were safe. Shouts from the darkness.

"Who's that?"
"It's me, Steve."
"Where's Eric?"
"Here I am."

We sat close together, closer than we normally did. Each of us told his story of the flames, the noise, the heat, or how close he had been to deploying his fire shelter. It had happened so fast.

I found a comfortable rock to lean against and pulled out a canteen for a drink. The water rippled inside, quivering, my hand shaking. We waited for the rest of the crew to arrive.

"Sonora, over here."

Several folks from our crew had mistakenly gone over to other crews. All crews look pretty much the same when you're staring up into the light from their headlamps. There were four crews in the beloved rockslide area. Ours was the last one there and definitely the most threatened. The others just got to watch a good fireworks show. (The year before, I had met an old-timer firefighter, and he had told me that when things go bad on a fire, the best thing to do — if you can — is just stand back and applaud the power of nature.) That's what these other crews had done. We had not had the luxury.

Four people from our crew were missing: the two

we had left behind, plus Henry and Alex, who had run back to make sure the others were okay, uncertain if they could reach the clearing before being overtaken by the wall of flames. I had never seen such courage. I tried to reach them on the radio. No response. I changed channels and tried again. Same results. Nothing. No static, no sound of voices, just silence.

Those of us on the rockslide could only sit back and watch the curtain of flames overrun the area where we knew they were, watching the pulsing, golden flames do their work, and wondering if, at that moment, some of our friends were dying.

Then, down below us, more flames erupted, hissing. We grabbed our gear in a hurry and moved even farther uphill. The burst of flames quickly went out. We settled down for keeps. Everybody spoke quietly, hushed, as if we were in a library. Or at a funeral.

I took out a mint chocolate chip granola bar from my chest pocket, something I had been saving for a special occasion, which this certainly was. I offered half to the person beside me, Brad, my squad boss. He was using the radio I had been carrying, and was not having any luck, either. He sounded so forlorn, calling the full names of Henry and Alex, over and over, with no response. In the background, the distant, thundering roar of the flames.

"Dammit, dammit, dammit!" I kept whispering to myself, over and over to myself though I don't know why, like a song going through my head without reason. I realized then, in that moment, in that rockslide, that a normal, rational person could, upon being exposed to something hideously sudden and horrible, go totally and irrevocably insane. Snap! Just like that, you could loose your marbles. Poof.

The smoke was worse. It always is once the flames die down but the smoldering trees remain. I put my red bandana over my nose and mouth, cowboy bankrobber style. It helped a little but did nothing for my eyes, squinting, watering. They were on their own.

During our Dash for Life, the terrific updrafts from the flames carried off the smoke, high into the night sky. In a fast-moving forest fire like this, for a flash the temperature will exceed 2,000-2,500 degrees. Almost as quickly, the flames pass by and the inferno heat is gone. Only the fragile exterior of the tree, the leaves, needles, and bark, is affected. Scrape away the half-inch charred layer and underneath is soft, gleaming wood. Chop into it with a pulaski and clear sap will ooze from the wound. For a while the tree continues to pump nutrients through its system, not yet aware that it is dead.

It had been 30 minutes since we'd found the rockslide, and the fire had just about had it. We shifted positions to watch the flames move east, but they died once they hit the ridge top. With nothing left to burn, that was the end of that. There one second, vanished the next. I was almost sad to see them disappear, knowing that things for me had changed, forever, the way I would look at my life, the way I would live my life. I felt that when the flames stopped so too would the changing process.

Only an occasional flareup could be seen, followed a second or two later by the "whoosh!" It took several seconds for the sound to reach us, the same delay between seeing lightning and hearing its thunder.

Division F

THE ROCKSLIDE was nothing but a huge, treacherous mass of unstable, jagged, fractured rock just waiting to gash a shin or injure an ankle. There was no dirt to stabilize it, either, just rock after rock after rock, ranging from lunchbox-sized to as big as a sofa. What a miracle it was that nobody had been hurt scrambling up the rockslide at full tilt!

We saw three people down below. As they entered the rockslide and slowly climbed closer, we recognized them as Henry, Alex and a division boss.

We mobbed Henry and Alex. "Pull up a rock!" The invitation was extended to the division boss as well. He sat a little removed from us, slowly munching an apple. He looked so sad, and didn't say much. I felt sorry for him. This hadn't really been his fault. How was anybody to know that something like this was going to happen? Henry said that everybody in the clearings — all 41 people — had used their fire shelters and was safe.

"Is that one guy going to put *this* in his resume?" somebody asked, laughing.

We sat around for another 45 minutes or so, savoring the sensation of breathing. It's really quite a nice sensation — breathing — when you get right down to it.

With everybody's headlamps turned off to conserve batteries, the smoky darkness enveloped the group. I drank heavily from my canteen, appreciating the smoothness of the water as it sloshed around in my mouth and eased down my throat. That felt great. It was two-thirty in the morning, but nobody was sleepy. Not a yawn — the residual adrenaline still drifting around in our bodies made drowsiness impossible.

I looked down at Alex. A deployed fire shelter was strapped to his field pack in a big, crinkling, metallic bundle. For some reason, I felt jealous. I guess I was caught up in the mystique of the Forest Service. Often times I had heard other firefighters remark, "Well if I ever have to use my shelter that will be *my* last fire, I'll tell you that." I longed for something tangible like that, to justify why, after three years of fire — each one getting riskier than the one before — I didn't want to do this much longer. Something that I could tell others, so they would not question.

Our orders came in over the radio: proceed back down the line, follow Sacaton Creek to some vehicles which would pick us up at 10 a.m. Dang! We were hoping for a helicopter ride out.

We eased into our packs, clicked our headlamps on, took our places in line, and set off. No use waiting around here. It took us almost ten minutes to carefully pick our way over the jumble of rocks. How we had climbed it at a run . . . how had we done that? We got to the bottom of the slide and said our goodbyes to the rocks. After searching for a moment we found the fireline. It headed south, through the heart of the burn. We would see what the inferno had done.

The light from our headlamps could only penetrate three or four feet. The smoke was too thick. It was like looking down one of those shouting cones used by cheerleaders at a football game, and in that thin shaft of light we could watch thousands of bits of ash swirl and drift around. Most of the time we couldn't see our feet. Our noses were running like crazy from the smoke. We could tell where everybody was by their sniffles and coughs.

After almost a half mile of the same we came to the spot where we had begun our Dash for Life. The smoke was thinner, and at times we could see fifty feet into the gloom. Smoldering logs cast their own light. Looking up at the charred, stripped trees — beautiful, vibrant evergreens the last time we had seen them — sent a chill down my back. The silence was overpowering. We had run a long way! If we had stopped during the Dash and decided to open our fire shelters we all would have been killed, just like the trees. Something had even happened to the rocks; they appeared to have changed color, having been subjected to such intense heat. We walked slowly through the dead forest. Too many new feelings struggling to be accepted, in too short a time to be understood.

We passed a hot "chimney" tree, hollow and on fire. The flames at the base rushed upwards, spurting out the top and spiraling through cracks in the sides. It looked as if it could fall at any time. We walked quickly past and kept a close eye on it. Several minutes later it did come crashing down, and missed Jerry by less than a yard. He was having a rough night.

We continued following the fireline (some good it had done!) with burned-out trees on all sides. Later, we found out that the fire had galloped over the line, reached the top of the ridge, and gone out on its own.

Several of the firefighters had managed to sprint over the ridge into the drainage on the other side, safe, but had deployed their fire shelters, just in case. They saw what they were up against.

It's tricky to know when to open your fire shelter; most firefighters never have occasion. It takes a moment to open and get into a fire shelter. You need to know when to stop and use it — that's the secret. If you keep running, desperate to find a safety zone, but get caught by the fire before you can open your shelter when you realize there *isn't* a safety zone, well, then it's all over. I know if I had turned around during the Dash and seen the folks behind me using their shelters, I probably would have used mine as well. As it was, we all just kept running, and wondering.

Should I use my shelter?

Should I run?

Is there a safety zone up ahead?

Where? Can we get there in time?

It seems to me that in most rational settings, the mind controls the function of the body, or so it appears. In a high stress environment — running from a raging forest fire, for example — the body seems to take over, saying to the mind, "Move over! *You're* the one who got us into this mess in the first place!" It is in these situations that it appears that the mind and body are acting totally independent of each other. Or is it that for the first time, they are truly united, acting as one, inseparable?

We kept walking, down that steep black elevator shaft area, which now didn't seem all that steep since we were going downhill instead of up. We left the burn, and walked for another 10 or 15 minutes before coming to a small clearing in the brush where we rested and regrouped. No sooner had we done that when a terrific roar of fire came from down below in the drainage. The sky brightened suddenly. Someone shouted, **"Here it comes again!"**

Down below, just like before — how stupid can we get! — the fire blasted through the brush. There was no safety zone nearby. We were really in a pickle, surrounded by heavy brush.

I tore off the buttons of my fire shelter pouch and took the shelter out, ready to open it. Then the flare-up died. We agreed to get the hell out of this place. I hurriedly put my shelter back in its case, hoping that nobody had seen me take it out. I saw several other people sheepishly doing the same thing.

To say that we moved briskly down the fireline is indeed an understatement. The footing was bad; smooth rock chutes covered by a light dusting of dirt, with some marble-sized pebbles thrown in for good measure. Every now and then somebody took a good tumble, but nobody bothered to holler out a score. Let's get off this mountain!

Finally, a safe place. The fire was across the drainage at about our same level, and we were nearly to Sacaton Creek.

We followed the streambed for about half a mile, passing the spot where the night before we had slept in our space blankets and built a small campfire to stay warm, back when fire was still our friend. It seemed so long ago.

Our crew moved aside to let the others go past. Many carried their fire shelters strapped to their packs. In the dim light of the sunrise I could see that some of the shelters were smoky gray, almost charred, while others looked like shiny new aluminum foil. The people carried them proudly. Most of these firefighters were Native Americans from northern New Mexico. They didn't look at us as they walked quickly past.

The rest of the walk seemed to go on forever, taking us past several old cabins and through a couple of barbed wire gates. We hadn't been this way before. We finally arrived at the spot where we were to be picked up. It was almost 9:30 in the morning. We had made good time coming out. No vehicles were waiting for us. The exhausted crews in front of us were already stretched out.

We filed past several large, loose piles of tools, pulaskis and shovels. Our crew moved to the side of the dirt road and sat down in a long line, taking off packs and leaning against the embankment. I took a swig of water and fell asleep.

That night after the flare-up, Jerry and I met a good friend of ours who used to work with us. Coincidentally, he had been assigned to work the first aid tent on this fire. We recognized him from a distance and went over to talk with him, waving. He smiled when he saw us.

"I heard you guys had a run-in last night," then he told us what it had looked like from fire camp, six miles away.

"I was working the night shift, seven p.m. to seven a.m., and it was really slow," he said. "A couple of blistered feet and small cuts and that was about all. It was real quiet in camp. I was in the tent." He motioned to the first aid tent behind him.

"At about 1 o'clock a whole bunch of calls came over the radio, like something really exciting was happening. I looked outside and jeez!, the whole mountain was on fire. Somebody asked if he should wake up everybody and I said, 'Yeah, you'd better!' Some guy in Overhead stepped out of his tent and just stood there, looking at the mountain. All he said was one thing, *'Son of a bitch!'* By then all the radios had gotten really quiet and the fire had sort of broken up into two parts, one branching to the right and the other to the left. Man, it was like the whole mountain was on fire. It really looked bad from down here. All we did was just stand around and watch it, not much else we could do. We knew there were crews in that area and we were wondering what was going on up there."

He moved a little closer to Jerry and me and lowered his voice.

"What was it like?"

Jerry looked up at the mountain and took a deep breath. "Do you really want to know?"

Mad-Dog Fire

(Third year of fire)

Division G

A MONTH had passed since the Haystack Fire. Jerry and I were at the door of the ranger station, heading out. Oscar had just answered the phone in his office. His shout from the back room stopped us in our tracks.

"Hold on just a minute there, guys!"

Uh oh.

"Maybe we should leave anyway," Jerry whispered, joking. "I didn't hear him ask us to wait, did you?"

A minute later we heard Oscar hang up the phone. He called to us through the wall. "You guys feel like going on a fire?" No reply from Jerry or me.

"You guys still there?" Oscar laughed.

"Yeah, still here. What's up?"

"There's a fire down near Benchmark. They want us to bring our engine there and help them out. How about it?"

We could tell where this conversation was going. We could tell where *we* were going, too.

The drive took a little more than two hours. As we approached Benchmark, Oscar used his hand-held radio to call their fire dispatcher. Driving with one hand, he leaned way out the window with his radio. His transmission would be nothing but static if he did not. The dispatcher gave us instructions to proceed directly to a place she pronounced "Too-lee." Our road map spelled it Touli. It was farther to the north about 30 miles. We went through Benchmark without stopping and continued on the interstate in our huge, flashy, lemon-yellow fire engine, rumbling down the highway, sitting high above all the passenger cars and trucks, waving to the little kids who stared at us from the back of their parents' car, feeling very firefighterish. Wasn't this every child's dream?

After many more "We know what we're doing and it's good to be a firefighter" salutes, the three of us pulled into Touli. It was nothing more than a massive truckstop, restaurant, and hotel. A large, spotted leopard paced back and forth in a tiny cage out by the gas pumps, to attract more people to buy gas, I guess.

From the parking lot we could see the fire to the east about a half mile away, burning in mixed grass, catclaw, and whatever else could eke out a living in these parts. The fire looked as if it would be a piece of cake. None of the truckers gave it a second glance.

Driving past the rows of semi-trucks, Oscar spotted a woman wearing a shiny black mini-skirt, high heels, and a ton of makeup. She was sashaying arm-in-arm with an excited, road-weary trucker, making a beeline for the hotel.

"Hey, it looks like we're just in time!" Oscar said, laughing. "Should I hit the siren?"

Naw. We crept through the parking lot in low gear, our engine suddenly seeming very puny against the backdrop of big rigs. The parking lot petered out but we kept going, following a narrow dirt road that seemed to be heading in the general direction of the fire. After going about half a mile, with the fire maybe a hundred yards off to our right and no other fire engines in sight, we turned around and headed back to the truckstop. Oscar called the dispatcher again on the radio, leaning way out the window. She said, "Continue on the interstate a couple more miles. You'll know when you get there."

Back on the interstate and waving to the kids, we tried to decide on a name for the fire. Wildfires are usually named after the most prominant natural or man-made feature in the area. We scanned the horizon for ideas, but there weren't many landmarks in this part of the country.

"Since we're having a little trouble figuring out how to get to the fire," Oscar observed, "why don't we just call it, 'The fire near a truckstop called Touli, pronounced "Too-lee," behind the parking lot and down a dirt road.'" Good suggestion, but the legal name of a fire is limited to 12 letters or less. We'd think of a good one later.

One of the volunteer fire department engines, ruby red and covered with dust, was waiting for us at the next turnoff. We followed it north down another dirt road. After several miles, we arrived at a herd of similar engines. The fire trucks stood nine feet tall at the shoulder. A couple of them were red, others white, and one was brown . . . a brown fire engine! I had never seen a brown fire engine before — I'll bet it had a story to tell! The volunteers were standing in front of the engines.

Oscar, Jerry, and I got out, slammed the doors, and sauntered over like hired guns, wearing matching, regulation, yellow, fire-resistant shirts; green pants, black leather boots, yellow hard hats, and gloves.

The volunteers wore tee-shirts, faded jeans, tennis

shoes or cowboy boots, and baseball caps advertising beer, chewing tobacco, or American-made trucks. We were greeted by the Fire Boss; around there they did not call them Incident Commanders. He gave us the briefing on the fire.

It was 400 acres and burning actively on the northeast flank, wind from the southwest. The blaze was surrounded by dirt roads. I liked the sound of that; it wasn't going anywhere. Our job was to hold a position on the east edge of the burn and make a series of running attacks on the fire with our engine if the fire got close to the road. A "running attack" is when the fire engine slowly drives beside or even behind the fire while a crewmember hoses down the flames as they go along, gradually extinguishing and encircling the blaze. The only problem was that our engine had a PTO, a Power-Take-Off style pump, meaning that the truck had to be stationary, in neutral, while pumping. Our truck's main engine powered the pump. It was great for putting out a large volume of water, on a house fire, for example, but absolutely worthless for running attack. The Fire Boss told us, "Well, do the best you can." The other fire engines would have to do the initial attack. All of them had smaller, centrifugal pumps, which worked independently of the main engine and were custom built for this dramatic running attack method.

"Anybody got any questions?" the Fire Boss asked. There were none. "Okay, then, let's go." We convoyed down the road, our shiny engine in the rear doing its best to keep up with the other engines as they tore off down the road.

Several l-o-n-g straightaways later, we located a nice, safe place to park the engine, in an overgrazed area without any vegetation whatsoever. The cows had eaten everything in sight.

"Looks like we got us a safety zone!" Oscar remarked, unrolling the hardline hose from the side of the engine facing the fire, just in case. Jerry and I, meanwhile, grabbed our initial attack gear and stuffed some fusees in our packs. Jerry took a shovel and recommended that I get a "flapper," a floppy, black rubber, smooth-sided, industrial-strength doormat firmly attached to the end of a heavy-duty rake handle. I had never used one of these flappers in combat before. They were designed to smother and flap out small flames in light grass, hence the name. Jerry said they worked really well.

Our plan was this: Jerry would use his shovel to scrape a quick scratchline, from which we would burn out using our fusees, with me following behind, using my flapper to extinguish our linear blaze and create a "blackline" which the main fire could not cross. It would stop the fire, dead. I was looking forward to this novel method of initial attack. It was going to be really slick. We would show these fellows how to fight fire!

It soon became evident that our surefire plan would not be necessary, however. Just as we were getting started, the wind shifted and our flank went out — on its own. In light fuels, a slight wind change, or even a narrow cow path, can halt the flames and even put them out entirely. Disappointed, Jerry and I went over where the fire had been burning only a minute before. It was time for mop-up. About the only thing that needed mopping-up were about a million cowpies, each of them sending up a thin, putrid, yellowish-gray wisp of smoke.

My flapper wasn't designed with cowpies in mind. In fact, it was totally worthless; I had met the enemy. I tried it on a smoking cowpie, just to see what would happen. I smacked the cowpie a good wallop and a billow of sparks swirled in the backwash of dusty air. Jerry leaned on his shovel, laughing. I told him that someday I would get him back for this. And actually, I still owe him, come to think of it.

The fire began to really heat up in a nearby brush-covered flat area. A pair of volunteer engines raced toward the hot spot. Jerry and I decided to watch the show.

"This is going to be good," Jerry noted.

The big, red engine in the lead turned off the road and sped cross-country, heading straight toward the flames without slowing down. Flames went up taller than the truck. The engine closed to within fifty feet of the flames, and then all heck broke loose.

Water began blasting from the four nozzles stationed strategically on the engine: one in front near the bumper, one on top toward the back, one on the rear fender, and one on the driver's side behind the cab. Each nozzle had a guy wearing a tee shirt and blue jeans behind it. They had no safety gear. Their only defense was water, and man! did they use their water!

Water sprayed all over the place. It was like watching a land-locked firefighting tugboat in action, one that had the whole ocean to work with. The truck charged head-on into the flames until it was lost from sight, the crackle of the fire drowned out by the revving engine as the wheels struggled for traction. Higher in pitch than the bedlam and, in fact, adding to it, was a creative mixture of hooting and hollering from all the crewmembers involved, and there were a lot of them. Their shouts diminished when the engine emerged from the flames.

Once the truck cleared the fire, it immediately turned and accelerated to make a pass from the rear. The driver wrestled with the steering wheel as if it were a live thing. The fellows on the nozzles braced! The truck went in again, and again, and again. It was incredible! Thick clouds of amber dust mixed with the black smoke. Frantic shouts!, the roar of the engine — the crackle of the flames!, and then . . . . It was all over. The flame front was out; completely, irrevocably, 100%, dead out.

The truck headed back for the road without further ceremony. The fellow on the back waved. We waved back. We must have looked pretty darned foolish out there, on foot, especially me and my limp flapper.

It was impossible to forget those geysers of water, at times gracefully rising above the bedlam, other times flailing frantically at the flames.

Almost casually, the red engine bounced its way back to the dirt road, met up with the other engine, and together they charged down the dirt road toward another, more distant, hot spot far to the north. Jerry and I made our way slowly over to where the truck had done its work.

The ground was a mess: wheel trenches and skid marks crisscrossed the area, mixed with blown-out pockmarks where one of the guys with a nozzle had sent a high-pressure torrent almost straight down into the ground. The cool smell of soggy, burned grass wafted over the trenches left by the spinning tires. We picked our way cautiously, awed, like two people coming across unexpected wreckage. There was nothing left for us to do. Somehow they'd even extinguished the cowpies.

Within an hour, we got a radio call from Oscar. He asked us to return to our engine. The fire was out, our mission was complete. We took off our gear at the engine, headed down the road, and joined the local firefighters at their engines. They were talking about going out for dinner at a Mexican food restaurant in Benchmark.

"Do you fellows want to go along?" they asked.

"Sounds good."

But first we had our debriefing.

The Fire Boss stepped forward. He said that the fire was contained and controlled, and we were being sent home. He thanked us for coming down, and extended the invitation of dinner. Oscar accepted for us, then cautiously volunteered that the National Park Service was not accustomed to suppressing wildfires in the vigorous manner we had just witnessed. The Fire Boss kicked at the dirt with the pointy end of his cowboy boots.

"Well, I'll tell ya', I've been fightin' fahr out here for twenty-some years, and if there's one thing I've learned, well, it's that you've just got to go out there and mad-dog 'em. Yep, just mad-dog 'em plain and simple. It's the only way to do it. Ya' know, I've been mad-dogging these fahrs for twenty-odd years, and I ain't never got anybody hurt. (pause)

"Nah, I take that back. Ol' Les over there —" he motioned to a fellow with a sheepish grin on his face. "Yeah, I guess there was that one time when Les got himself a little bit hurt on a fire. I think it was that fire down near Juniper, wasn't it Les?" Les nodded silently, glancing around, embarrassed.

"Yeah, that's where it was, down near Juniper," the Fire Boss continued. "We was mad-dogging this fahr, I was drivin', Les was riding shotgun, and we drove into the flames, just like here. Thing was, though, we drove through this big, fluffy pile of grass, and this big ol' puff of flame came in the window and sort of burned Les on the ear, and his neck, and a little bit on his face." The Fire Boss brushed his pants with the flat of his hand. "That was a funny one, wasn't it Les?"

This fire near a truckstop called Touli, pronounced

"Too-lee," behind the parking lot and down a dirt road, now had a name. We climbed into our trucks and convoyed into town. We sat around at a big table and ate dinner. It was good Mexican food, and they were nice fellows.

We talked a lot about the Mad-Dog Fire.

Nail Canyon Burn

(Second year of fire)

Division H

"Are you going to turn it around and back in?" I asked.

"Naw," Brett replied casually, driving our Model 20 Forest Service engine down the road into Nail Canyon. He was the engine foreman.

"There's no need to. It's not like this is a real fire or anything."

His confidence was far from reassuring. Ever since Brett had come on board at the beginning of the season, it seemed that unusual and unexpected things had occurred in quick succession, one after the other. First, our engine underwent an unexplainable seige of flat tires, quickly turning us all into experts in the fine art of tire removal and repair. Then the truck's small, five-horsepower centrifugal pump developed a series of mysterious short-circuits, electrifying the pump unit so it gave you a terrific electric jolt if you touched it while it was running.

Catastrophe-in-progress surrounded Brett like a discernible cloud. It wasn't that he was such a bad guy; just a little lonely, perhaps.

We were headed for the Nail Canyon Burn. The district had been planning it for a while. We were going to ignite a prescribed fire and burn off the sagebrush that filled the bottom of Nail Canyon. Later on, somebody was going to come and re-seed it with grass. The long-term idea was to eliminate the sagebrush, re-establish the grass cover as palatable forage, and then allow the local ranchers to bring their cows in and eat it. Hmm.

All the available engines on the district were there. Ten firefighters, including Brett and me, had been called to help out. We were the last ones to arrive. It was ten o'clock in the morning.

We pulled in and parked facing down Nail Canyon, between the two other engines. One was a green Model 20 engine that was just like ours, with four-wheel drive and 200 gallons of water. The other engine was affectionately known as the Beast, a monster of a fire engine with 600 gallons sloshing around in its tank and over a mile of fire hose stacked in the back. It dominated the dirt parking area — ancient, monolithic.

"They don't make them anymore like the Beast, thank goodness," somebody had told me the year before, when I had worked as a crewmember on it.

Truly, the hulking presence of the Beast did little to reassure those of us who knew its legacy, how its motor drank almost a quart of oil each day; how a quick peek under the chassis revealed a haphazard collage of repairs, with jerry-rigged duct tape, baling wire, and even strips of cotton and rubber fire hose holding the Beast together.

Many years earlier, the Beast, with its high-volume, PTO pump, had stalled on a fire in Utah. This meant not only was the truck unable to move, but also the pump wouldn't work! Here they were, the fire approaching rapidly and the main motor going "rrr...rrr...rrr" at each turn of the key. The frantic crewmembers inside kept at it — "C'mon, baby, c'mon!" — until the quick-moving fire emerged from the forest and swept into the dry grass meadow. The crewmembers sprinted down the road and leaped aboard another engine as the fire burned completely around and under the Beast, leaving the recalcitrant engine intact but temporarily too hot to touch.

Yes, the presence of the Beast at the Nail Canyon Burn was far from comforting, and with Brett confidently stating, "It's a good day to burn!" we had a hunch that things might not go according to plan.

Jack, the Beast's foreman, had made a point of turning around and backing it in — going by the book — in case things suddenly went bad and he needed to leave fast.

I had never done any prescribed burning before, and was really looking forward to it. Everybody made it sound like a lot of fun: determining the time and place of the burn; planning the ignition patterns, the placement of the engines, and the safety zone. It's like playing real-life chess, and you decide where all the pieces go at the outset. The only thing not completely under your control is what the fire will ultimately do. That's the only drawback.

"Anybody want to help do the burning?" Gary, in charge of the burn, asked us.

"Sure, I'll help," I volunteered, being the only one to say anything. Gary gave me a handful of fusees, then lit his drip torch with a pocket lighter.

"Let's just see how it does," he announced, tipping a stream of liquid fire from the nozzle onto an unfortunate sagebrush on the edge of the parking area. Fire trickled over the top branches and gathered at the base of the knee-high bush, flared to waist height, and consumed the entire plant in less that a minute, leaving only six inches or so of the plant's shaggy, smoking stalk as a reminder.

"Looks good," noted Brett.

"Yeah, it does. You ready, Eric?" Gary asked, nodding at the fusees.

"Ready." I peeled the cap off one and struck the flint pad against the flare. On the third strike it caught. An orange plume jetted out the end. I took the cap off another and jammed the fusee headfirst into the handle of the burning one. That way, I wouldn't have to bend over as far to ignite the base of the bushes.

Gary and I headed away from the vehicles. "We'll keep about fifty feet apart, touch off some brush every fifteen feet or so, making zig-zags. That way the fire won't get too hot," he instructed. If the fire built up a head of steam — something we were trying to avoid — then the blaze would incinerate the brush right down to ground level, burning so hot it would sterilize the topsoil and then nothing would grow for a long time, not even with grass seeds sprinkled on top.

Gary led the way down Nail Canyon, walking due west through the brush. The canyon was several hundred yards wide, lined with jagged limestone walls that reflected the summer heat. A narrow dirt road ran generally down the middle of the canyon. What Gary had in mind was burning the north side of the canyon floor for half a mile, then crossing over the road and burning out the other side, coming back toward the engines. He tipped the drip torch, poured out a stream of fire, paused to watch the results, and then, satisfied, took several more paces and did it again. I was on his right, going a little slower. It took longer to get the bushes burning with my fusee.

We worked steadily westward, going farther into the canyon. Gary used the drip torch with a confidence that I envied. He had been in fire for years, and had a calm, friendly manner. He was very comfortable around fire. He dealt with fire the way a good cowboy manages his horse: fair, in control, and at ease.

The slight wind was in our faces, so the smoke blew away from us. The fellows back at the engines coughed loudly for effect, shouting through the flames, "Would you mind doing something about the smoke!"

The small ignition points slowly burned toward each other. A glance over my shoulder a few minutes later revealed an eight-foot high wall of orange flames following obediently behind us, thirty yards distant. Our fire crackled and swooshed. It was pretty. The engines crept down the road a hundred yards behind us and off to the left. Several fellows holding a nozzle apiece walked in the brush beside the Model 20's, doing some very low-key running attack by hosing down the flank of the fire so it wouldn't get going and threaten to cross the road.

At the end of the green procession came the Beast, its broken backup warning beeper emitting a steady warble as the truck eased along in reverse; Jack was really going by the book. He leaned way out the window, craning his neck, trying to see around the Beast and keep from accidentally backing into anything valuable, tucking back inside the cab and staring intently at the side-view mirror when his neck got tired. Both Model 20's were coming down the road headfirst.

An hour went by. Sagebrush burst into flames one-by-one. The sun eased overhead. The summer day started to warm up.

"Feel the humidity dropping?" Gary asked, calling above the steady snapping of our fire.

"Yeah, it sure is."

"If it gets much drier we'll have to quit burning."

"Okay."

"As long as the wind's from the west we'll be okay for now."

As if the breeze understood what he'd just said, it

paused, gusted several times, reconsidered and paused again, then confidently switched directions. Now it was blowing at us from the back. That's where our fire was, behind us, torching off sagebrush with gusto.

"Hey, Eric, let's hold off on the burning and see what the wind's going to do." Eight-foot flames at our backs, no longer burning into a headwind but instead encouraged by a tailwind, rose up to ten feet and seemed to enjoy the view. Our fire was burning noticeably hotter than only a moment before, especially along the canyon's northern margin.

"I think we should head back to the road," Gary announced. "The fire's getting a little too hot."

Back at the road, we took a quick swig of water from our canteens, and paused to look at our handiwork. The fire was now burning on its own accord, self-sustaining. It had momentum. It didn't need us any longer. I got the impression it just wanted us to leave it alone. A hundred yards up the canyon, the trio of engines marched single file toward us on the road. My engine was in the lead, with the men manning the nozzles concentrating on keeping the aggressive flames at bay. The fire rose higher than the fellows' heads, orange flames lashing at the powder-blue sky. Greasy black smoke billowed in sheets out of the canyon and over the south rim.

A sudden "whoosh!" to the north made me stop watching the smoke. Clusters of sagebrush erupted into thick tentacles of flame and launched a run along the base of the canyon wall. It charged through the brush as if in a race, distancing itself from the main body of fire, leaving hot, continuous flames in its wake, covering a hundred yards in no time at all. Apparently satisfied, it fishhooked to the left and let the wind drive it toward the road. I watched it, impressed.

"Look at it go," Gary said quietly, almost to himself. The burn wasn't going quite as he wanted. He and I both knew if the fire kept this up, it would soon approach the road, hit it at almost a right angle, and cross it in a flash, effectively separating Gary and me from one of our safety zones.

"I don't like the looks of that," Gary mentioned, watching it intently, without blinking. "Why don't you go ahead and get rid of your fusee."

Fusees are mighty hard to extinguish. I threw it overhand into the burn. It tumbled end-over-end — a flaming baton trailing carwheeling loops of smoke, vanishing into the wall of flames.

The breeze blew stronger. It smelled heavily of smoke. We were getting 12-foot flames now. Smoke flowed across the road between us and the engines.

The fire took on a nebulous, almost seductive aura of danger. One by one, it seemed to be taking away our options. It was calling the shots now, and we were basing our actions on its, not the other way around, as it should be. Only a few moments earlier, everything had looked so good, but now —

The fire intensified. Back at the engines, the fellows gave up trying to control the flames near the road and were hurriedly dragging fire hose back to the engines, carrying sloppy bundles of it in their arms. Smoke blowing across the road almost obscured them from view.

A roar from downstream. The fire dashed for the road and without pausing jumped it in one leap. Smoke surrounded us. We needed to get out of there.

"Which way?" Gary asked, blowing out the tip of his driptorch. I knew he already had the answer, but wanted me to figure it out on my own — quickly. He knew this was how a young firefighter builds confidence.

I could see that the fire downstream was dashing for the canyon wall. Tearing through the waist-high sagebrush, it would definitely beat us there. We could not climb out of the canyon, either. It was too steep. That left us one way out.

"Back toward the engines!"

"Good choice, let's go!"

Gary had injured both his knees while firefighting years before, but they didn't seem to bother him very much. He and I ran at 3/4 speed on the road, but then the fire ahead and off to the left got too hot as it bore down on the road, forcing us into the brush off to the right. Gauntlets of flame reached across the road, searching for a handhold on our side. The wind picked up, carrying enough smoke to completely obscure the engines. I took comfort knowing that they waited in front of us with a thousand gallons of water among the three of them. It was a good feeling, knowing they were there. Smoke from the swirling fire blotted them out again. We ran for the smoke. It lifted for a second and-

What was this? I couldn't believe my eyes!

The engines were leaving us behind!

Jack, in the big lumbering Beast, led the way, no doubt praying to himself, "Beast!, you'd better not stall! C'mon, don't stall!"

The fire was headed right for both Model 20's, but they were having trouble turning around, getting caught up in the heavy brush.

Smoke suddenly blew across the road so they were lost from view. Gary and I sprinted through gaps in the sage. It was open-field running at its finest. Gary held onto the drip torch like a football.

The smoke lifted. One Model 20 had completed the desperate maneuver, churning up huge billows of dirt with its tires, screeching. It sped up the road, following the Beast and trailing a 50-foot length of fire hose out the back. But something was wrong with my fire engine. It's motor was howling at maximum RPM but the tires weren't moving. It was in neutral! There was a commotion near the front bumper. Somebody was yelling and waving his arms, jumping up and down. Whoever was driving accidentally tooted the horn. The truck suddenly lurched backwards and stalled. It restarted and shrieked into gear.

Smoke and flames blew across our escape route. The fire had crossed the road! It was making its run, we were making ours, both racing for an imaginary point where our routes intersected. Whoever made it there first was the winner.

The smoke swirled and lifted again for a second. Somehow my engine had completed its turn and was scooting up the road, also trailing a 50-foot length of fire hose from the back. The metal nozzle on the end hopped and jumped down the road. Goodbye.

We were on our own.

One final glimpse of the retreating engine and then

it was gone. We hurdled the bushes instead of going around. A fantastic, whooshing roar came from the fire. It was playing for keeps now. We ducked into the curtain of smoke. Flames lunged out of the top, almost directly above us.

"Keep going!" Gary yelled. "Almost there!"

I held my hand over my cheek to shield it from the heat. We couldn't see where we were going. Heavy smoke, total blackout — five yards, ten yards, fifteen yards. Better not be a barbed wire fence in our way!

Suddenly we emerged from the wall of smoke. The heat and the smoke and the whoosh of the flames were suddenly behind us. It was sunny and bright on the other side. We headed for the road, slowing to a dog-trot when we reached it. The engines had gone a hundred yards up the road and then circled the wagons.

We walked the rest of the way to the vehicles. Gary set the drip torch in the back of the closest truck with a loud clunk and announced, "Hey guys, thanks for waiting."

"You bet," somebody replied, preoccupied, busy listening to one of the other fellows talking quickly about the turnaround fiasco. The fellow doing most of the talking had been driving my engine. He was a rookie, who, in the panic, had somehow ended up behind the wheel, with Brett in the passenger seat.

"All I can remember is Kevin," he said, swallowing hard, slightly breathless.

"Man, here comes the fire, and Kevin's jumping up and down in front of the truck!, pounding his fists on the hood like a gorilla, shouting at me through the windshield, **'Turn it around! Get this son of a bitch turned around!'"**

This was *exactly* what I'd been telling Brett from the very beginning, Mr. "It's not like this is a real fire." When I saw him leaning on the hood of our engine, casual, nodding, I couldn't help but smile.

Meadow Creek Fire

(Second year of fire)

Division I

We were on standby.

We'd already been two days playing pickup basket-ball games at a high school gymnasium in McCall, Idaho, and I was getting tired of it. I knew if I had to listen to another full day of that dang basketball — thump..thump..thump — I was going to draw a big foul.

We'd just had breakfast. Our crew boss came by to give us our morning briefing.

"Anybody want to go standby at the heliport? If you do, at least there's a chance you'll get sent out on a fire. It's either that," he paused significantly, "or this." Somebody threw him a ball. He dribbled it once.

"So who wants to volunteer?"

My hand went up as if it had a mind of its own. Several other folks volunteered, too. We were told to get all of our gear together, pack up, change out of our gym shorts and sneakers, and be ready to leave in half an hour.

Within an hour we were unloading our gear at the heliport, just off the main runway at McCall's municipal airport. There were nine of us. We were all in the same boat: "Initial attack/helitack standby." Our foreman divided us into three mini-squads, three people each, available for immediate helicopter dispatch should there be a call for fresh people on a remote fire somewhere. Three people are able to handle a small lightning fire that pops up unexpectedly.

I was in Team One. Three jet helicopters were lined up in front of us, ready to go. A crewmember asked our weights and wrote them down on her clipboard. She told us to get comfortable.

"Stand by," she said.

"We're getting good at that," somebody remarked.

We spent the next 12 hour shift eating oranges, playing cards, talking, sleeping, or reading about lost tribes of Amazon pygmies in back issues of "National Geographic."

The next day it was the same story, saying "So long!" to the poor folks cooped up in the gymnasium

— talking loudly over the dribbling and drumming basketballs — then arriving at the heliport and preparing to stand by. More oranges, Go Fish, and old magazines.

And then I saw the airplane.

It had been there the day before, a slurry bomber. I asked the crew boss if I could go check it out.

"Is your gear all ready to go?"

"Yep, all ready."

"Sure, go ahead."

It turns out the plane was grounded for repairs. The pilot was doing some of the work, and he gave me a quick tour. He said that several days before he'd been sent aloft on a bombing mission with a full load of slurry, but the plane had developed a minor problem. Shortly after takeoff, one of the bomb bays had malfunctioned and 500 gallons of bright orange fire retardant had spilled out and plastered a farmhouse at the end of the runway. It did a job on the house; it needed several new windows, and some new shingles to replace those torn off by the slurry. It also needed new paint.

The pilot chuckled, wondering out loud what it must have been like to have been inside the house, one moment watching television and listening to a big plane take off, the next having the house sound as if it were coming apart at the seams.

The broken bay door on the tanker was still hanging open. Slurry dripped off the hinges and pooled on the tarmac. I bent down, and dipped my fingers into the mixture. It was orangish-red, sort of sticky yet slimy, about the consistency of really heavy-grade motor oil.

Most slurry bombers are World War II or Korean War vintage. This particular model carried 2,000 gallons of slurry in four bays, each holding 500 gallons. The term he used was "door." The pilot could drop one, two, three, or all four "doors" in a single pass. He said the slurry averaged $10.75 per gallon, including fuel, insurance, maintenance, slurry, and pilot costs — up to $20,000 for one full bomber mission!

It weighed just under ten pounds per gallon, slightly heavier than water. They dropped it going at least 180 miles per hour, from an altitude of "around 200 feet."

"Above the ground or above the trees?" I asked. He just smiled, a smile I would remember.

I paused to imagine a 500 gallon drop; a streaming, swirling, 5,000 pound, low-altitude, crimson mass traveling 200 miles an hour.

"You don't *ever* want to get caught in a slurry

drop," he warned. I recalled a picture I saw once at a Forest Service ranger station of a massive, 600 gallon, six-passenger, Model 71 fire engine that had accidentally been caught in a drop zone. The force of the slurry had ripped off the light bar on top, torn off both heavy-duty side mirrors, and caved in the roof. All the windows were blown out, too. There had been a crewmember inside when it happened. He was seriously injured by the flying glass and the concussion inside the cab. I'd also heard rumors of other smaller fire engines being totaled by a direct hit from a load of slurry. Getting caught in a drop zone is definitely to be avoided.

I was still on standby so I hurried back to the heliport. All of us there grabbed an early lunch. We'd just finished when the girl on the helitack crew came trotting around the corner of the command trailer, carrying her clipboard.

"Team One, you're up! Let's go! Get your gear and follow me!" My heart skipped a beat or two. I grabbed my gear. Within three minutes we were strapped into a sleek, red, helicopter. The turbine engine took hold and whined behind us. Wow, how quickly things change!

I had a window seat on the copilot's side. Actually, it was more than a mere window seat; the entire door had been removed and I could lean out of the heli-copter if I wanted, which I didn't. In a minute we were airborne. We passed low over the outskirts of McCall, Idaho, gaining elevation and heading east, straight into the heart of the vast River of No Return Wilderness. From our high and mighty perch, we could see a handful of large fires burning in the rugged mountains, the smoke rising densely into the hazy blue sky. We flew fairly low over one of the fires, and could see that nobody was trying to put it out. Was this our fire?

We flew on. I guess not. They were letting this one burn.

Straight ahead in the distance we could just barely make out an old, white, wooden lookout cabin. There was a small, four-acre forest fire burning just to the west of it. We approached, slowing, descending. The pilot pointed vigorously at the blaze and then pointed at us. He circled twice and touched down in a clearing near the cabin. We had arrived at the Meadow Creek Fire.

Division J

OUR MISSION was to save the old lookout cabin. The Forest Service is really gung-ho when it comes to protecting structures or houses of any type. Trees that burn up never write nasty letters to high-ranking Congressmen; people whose homes are destroyed by a forest fire often do.

Jack, the Incident Commander, mentioned that a slurry bomber was going to be coming in a few minutes to drop a full load on the fire to cool it off. There would be a lead plane guiding it in. The bomber was going to hit the north flank of the fire, and since that was the designated drop zone, I should avoid working in that area. Jack asked me to go downhill and work on a hot spot near the bottom of the burn, at the west end, farthest from the cabin.

"Do what you can, but watch out for the bomber."
I went by myself. The drifting, swirling smoke was
pretty thick. My eyes were watering badly by the time
I got down to the bottom of the burn.

I went to work with my shovel. Maybe 15 minutes
later, far away in the distance, I heard a heavy, dull
droning. Slurry bomber! The noise came closer.
Guiding the bomber in was a speedy, twin-engine lead
plane. Its job was to test the winds and show the
bomber where to drop. Lumbering behind was the
heavy, awkward, four-engine bomber, similar to the
one I'd seen earlier at the airport.

Both planes circled the fire for five minutes, then
the lead plane separated itself from the other plane
and began making several low passes right over the
center of the fire, going south-to-north. It was desig-
nating the drop zone, cutting through the central part
of the fire — the part which was burning the hottest.
The bomber would follow this south-to-north flight
line. I assumed the original plans for a drop on the
fire's extreme north flank had been scrubbed. I was in
a secure area 100 yards below the drop zone, but even
so I made my way over to a big boulder and ducked
behind. This would be my safety zone, just in case the
drop went amiss. Then I broke out my camera and got

ready to watch the show. This was going to be good! It's hard to take good pictures on a fire: you're either too busy working, or too busy running.

Way off in the distance, the two planes made their final, sweeping, descending left turn as they lined up for the drop. Then they were lost from sight behind the heavy trees. I waited . . . and waited.

Suddenly, the lead plane burst into view over the trees. No warning, just poof! there it was. Then came the booming roar of the bomber. I couldn't see it yet but I sure could hear it. The lead plane whipped by, going right-to-left. The bomber followed close behind, its thunder shaking the ground.

One of its "doors" suddenly snapped open and a thick mass of red retardant plunged from the belly, great globs of it shooting past in front of me at race-car speed, streaming a heavy, crimson mist hundreds of feet long. It plastered trees and smashed into a nearby rockslide. Wow! I couldn't believe how powerful it was!

Just as quickly, the planes were gone. Silence. My heart was beating like mad. I fumbled with the camera. I had taken one quick picture of the drop, but the noise had scared me so much I cowered behind the rock. Dang! That was awesome!

The lead plane made another, higher pass over the

drop zone to survey the damage, and I knew they were going to drop another load. I decided to sit tight, secure behind the rock, and get ready. This time I knew what to expect. The picture of the next drop was going to be a great one.

Off in the distance I could again see the planes lining up for the drop zone. They vanished behind the trees and a minute later, sure enough, here they came! Again, the sudden vroom! of the lead plane blasting past, and then the earth-shaking roar of the bomber. Again the drop — a bit earlier than the last — only this time I was ready with the camera, the bomber centered in the viewfinder. Yeah! The folks back home will love to see this!

The second load of slurry came out thicker than the first one. Rather than spilling from the bay in a continuous sheet, it just came out all at once, a big, goopy mass of high-speed slurry. It dispersed somewhat but there were still large globs of it — the size of basketballs — that hit the ground intact. They punished the rocks with a vengeance, splattering violently into a thick mist. I could smell the slurry. It had a scent all its own: earthy, slightly toxic, like mildew.

I lost sight of the planes for several minutes, and began to think that maybe that was the end of the show. Wrong. High overhead went the lead plane and the bomber, only now they went from east-to-west, a change from their previous north-to-south pattern. Hmmm, what was this?

A minute later, the lead plane came low overhead, going east-to-west in a single pass, over the spot where Jack had mentioned he wanted the original drop zone. It passed directly overhead, and that was not good. If the bomber dropped only a second or two late, the slurry would carry over the drop zone and hit my present position. Adrenaline started to kick in.

I decided to get the heck out of there, and headed south. Dog-trotting, I contoured through the burned area, looking over my shoulder for the planes. I couldn't see them, but I could hear them out there, somewhere.

Where was everybody else? Then I heard voices yelling far above me, an occasional piercing whistle mixed in. Oh, I get it; they're worried about me and want me to join them by the guard station!

"Coming!" I replied. "I'm on my way!" I began to trot uphill. Everything was going to be just fine.

I was almost halfway to the top of the hill. The going was slow and unsteady. I kept slipping on the fresh slurry from the previous drops. It was a mess. To my right was a huge rockslide; to my left, the fire, the old drop zone, and lots of trees that were having a bad day. Straight ahead, my companions awaited.

"VROOM!" The lead plane whipped over the rock-slide on my right and passed overhead, low and fast. I instinctively ducked, taken totally by surprise. What was it doing? What was going on?

The rumble of the bomber . . . I looked to my right . . . "Oh no!" here it came! charging into sight. It seemed to take a bead on me.

I'm in the drop zone! The picture of that squashed Model 71 engine, a victim of slurry, flashed through my mind.

DAMN!

There was only enough time to throw my shovel away, and dive onto the rocks, no time to wonder about what would happen next. The roar of the bomber was incredible, shattering. I cringed on the rocks, belly down. Then, above the roar of the airplane I heard a strange metallic "pop-pop!", the sound of two bomb bays as they burst open. This was immediately followed by a sound I can't really describe, a loud, weird, hissing noise — the sound of 1,000 gallons of slurry as it ripped through the air, a horizontal mass moving at 200 mph.

I closed my eyes and held on.

In a fraction of a second the whole world turned into slurry. Slurry smashed into the rocks around me.

Slurry smashed into me, pounding my legs and back with heavy, gummy sludge. It hurt. A big glob hit me on the side. Sharp, ripping noises came from the trees as the slurry tore off branches overhead.

Even before I knew what I was doing, I found myself up and running; tripping, slipping, and stumbling on the slick-coated rocks. I fell. I stared over my left shoulder in amazement at broken branches and torn pieces of bark raining down. Several dead trees had been knocked completely over. Holy cow, I'd been in that! The air was heavy with a slurry mist. Slurry dripped and trickled off the remaining branches and coursed down the trunks of the trees, rivers of the stuff running down the slope. It tasted awful.

I couldn't break stride and slow down. I noticed the shovel gripped in my sticky glove, but didn't remember picking it up.

By the time I topped out near the cabin I had slowed to an awkward, soggy walk. I was exhausted.

"What happened to you?" were the first words to greet me. Then one guy, a fellow I never really cared for, said, "I knew that was going to happen to you. I just *knew* it!" Finally, somebody asked, "Are you okay?" I nodded, and coughed out, "Yeah, I think so." I didn't really want to talk, my voice was shaking so badly. In fact, my whole body was shaking, and my knees felt as if they could give out at any time. A couple of the guys started to laugh, but I cut that short with a "Dammit, its not funny!" because it wasn't. Didn't they realize that I could have been killed? Didn't they realize what it's like to get caught in a slurry drop? How stupid can you get, laughing at a guy who feels like wetting his pants. Give me a break!

It took a while to even begin to calm down. I walked around aimlessly, trying to relax, but feeling very tired and old. I'd never gone through anything like this before. Who has? I felt like lying down, but my heart kept racing, so I just kept walking around, muttering "Dammit!" under my breath.

Less than three hours before, at the airport, I had dipped my fingers into the slurry and thought, "Isn't this interesting." Now I was out in the middle of nowhere, covered with the stuff. I had slurry under my hard hat, up my shirt, in my ears, on the inside of my glasses.

A nice fellow named Tom came over and asked if he could take my picture for his scrapbook. I liked Tom.

"Sure."

We found a suitable spot near the cabin, and I posed with my shovel. It was the only thing holding me up. He asked me to turn around and get the back. I looked out at a lone pine tree, and took a deep breath. Dammit. It was the only thing I could think of to say.

Tom asked if I was sure I was okay, and I said yeah, just a bit shaken up. He said he could understand why. He said he had taken several pictures of the bomber from up near the cabin, almost looking down on the airplane.

It was a heck of a show!" he said. "Must have been something to be in it."

Division K

AT DUSK, Tom and I teamed up to mop-up the fire's south flank. I could handle this. We found a small patch of smoldering duff, surrounded on two sides by rocks, and though it was burning very slowly, we decided to put in a quick scratchline. Nothing fancy or pretty, just a narrow scrape around the burning area to keep it from spreading.

Tom and I were working under a huge, fat, half-dead tree, its draping branches brushing our hard hats. Without warning, the tree tremored slightly, a "Pop!" sounded from the trunk, and it began to fall on us. Tom yelled, "Lookout!" We bailed out. I went left, he went right.

The tree wedged on another tree and didn't crash into the ground like most falling snags do. Rather, it bent the other tree down and came to rest partially on the ground, some of its thick branches breaking off under the weight.

"Tom! Tom, are you all right!" Where was he?

"Yeah, I'm okay!" His voice came from far away on the other side of the rockslide — how he managed to get way over there so fast I'll never know! When I told him later about how fast he must have moved, he said, "I figured I had to get *away* from there."

It took me another couple minutes to calm down from that near hit. Two of them within an hour! My nerves were nearly shot.

We took a short break for dinner up in the guard station, then went back out to mop-up for a while. The fire was history. The slurry drop had really done it in. With the thick smoke still drifting around, the darkness was total, broken only by our dim headlamps or an occasional remnant of flickering flame. We moved like ghosts through the haze, alone or in pairs, calling to each other through the blackness. It's funny how ineffective one's vision is in these times, yet how clearly the sound of a voice, or a tool clanking off the rocks, carries. Other sounds were also heard that night, the sound of falling trees. Snags. We call them "widowmakers," and there's a reason for that.

The smoldering hillside was quite steep, with a pitch of about thirty degrees. That might not sound too bad, but when you walk up and down it six or seven times it's definitely steep. And the word "hillside" does not quite give the right impression, either. No. "Hillside" has a peaceful, relaxed connotation, one of children playing tag and rolling in the grass as butterflies drift past, while Mom and Dad hold hands and fly a kite.

No, this was not a hillside. Call it a rocky slope and leave it at that. Good, honest dirt was a rare find in the tangle of loosely-piled rocks and scree. I wondered how all these trees got here in the first place, but somehow they did manage to grow in abundance. They were mainly lodgepole pine, known especially for their usefulness as telephone poles. To firefighters in the forest, they also mean something else.

Trouble.

Because, when a typical lodgepole pine matures and later begins to fall into decay, a strange thing happens. The base of the tree, its source of strength and support, gradually begins to weaken and rot. Its fire-resistant bark sloughs away, leaving the vulnerable heartwood underneath exposed to the elements. Wood-eating insects find this arrangement particularly attractive, and quickly set to work, tunneling happily into the pulpy mass. The tree becomes weak, vulnerable. The older it is, the weaker it gets. A breeze can blow a tree over, snapping it off at ground level. A strong gust can take them out by the score.

And if one day a bolt of lightning — firefighters call them "cash bolts" because they bring overtime money and hazard pay — ignites a small, four-acre fire in the mountains of central Idaho, it burns through the rocky undergrowth, occasionally flaring up to torch a lodgepole pine like a huge match. The smoldering continues for days. The trees weaken. The rotted fibers at ground level slowly burn and get weaker and weaker.

Then along comes a slurry bomber, and people working on the hill. It grows dark and they break for dinner. They return to work on the rocky slope and a gentle breeze begins to blow.

Tom and I were working after dinner, mopping-up a hot spot on the perimeter of the fire. The slurry on my shirt had dried into a semi-brittle shell — stiff, pink, and ugly. I felt the breeze and took out my windbreaker. The breeze passed softly through the trees, pure and peaceful. Tom was working off to the side. Then I heard another sound, a faint, tentative creaking, followed immediately by a sharp "pop!" That was all: "creeeek-pop!" What was that? It sounded a lot like the tree that nearly fell on Tom and —

Out of the darkness came a tremendous, earth-shaking crash as a tree uphill smashed into the rocks. Branches broken off by the plunge bounced and skittered far downhill. Wow, that was close! Was anybody working up there? Somebody yelled a quick rollcall, to see if everybody was okay. We were.

We couldn't see anybody — a dark night, the smoke. I stood still for a minute, shaken and surprised, and then realized why someone had once told me, "If you ever get sent to Idaho on a fire, watch out for the snags. Those lodgepole pine will get you."

I went back to work, listening to the steady clanking of Tom's pulaski somewhere off to my right. Later, another tired "creeeek" came from somewhere uphill. Again, the thunderous crash.

It was so dark, with the swirling smoke blotting out even the bare outline of the trees, that you would never see a tree until it was right on top of you. Right on top of you. What am I doing out here, anyway?

We kept working, every nerve in our bodies tingling in anticipation. No longer did I feel tired.

We all tried to work near a big rock — any big rock, it didn't matter which one — anything to dive behind if we had to. No longer did I think continuously about the roar of the slurry bomber and the hiss of the retardant slicing through the air. I had other things to worry about now. Which tree was going to fall next? Which way was it going to go?

Above me on the slope, another groaning "creeeek," sounding like the door opening into a haunted mansion. Then came a short cough, almost human, as the holding wood gave out. A faint sigh, increasing in intensity, as the tree fell and its branches cleaved the nightime air. Running, leaping in the opposite direction, I cowered behind a rock. From behind me came the resounding crash. The sound echoed off the rocks and trees.

The remainder of the shift was spent dodging unseen and sometimes imaginary falling trees. Nobody counted how many trees fell that night. It really didn't matter, all it took was one.

It was just shy of 2 a.m. when Jack rounded us up.

"Let's call it a night." We trudged up the hill to sleep for a few hours in the cabin.

I lay down in my sleeping bag and couldn't help but think about what had happened that day. Waking up to the sound of basketballs, eating oranges at the airport, talking with a pilot while he fixed his plane. A helicopter ride, a slurry bomber, falling trees.

I didn't sleep at all. It just never came. My heart

raced all night. It averaged 140 beats a minute. What was happening to me?

Then it was dawn. The sky lightened in the east. The sun came up over the tall trees of Idaho. Another day.

Rattlesnake!

Division L

FOUR OF my friends have been bitten by rat-tlesnakes.

One was nailed by a timber rattlesnake in the leg and went blind for a while, spending some time in the hospital. He recovered, but never really wanted to talk about it very much.

The other fellow was Fred, full of vim and vigor - seeking daring exploits as many young men do. One day he noticed a small rattler lying off in the grass.

"It was a *real* tiny rattlesnake, not much bigger than this," he demonstrated, holding both hands less than a foot apart. One of his thumbs had a small scar on top.

"I thought it was really interesting, this rattlesnake lying in the grass. I guess that's probably what rattlesnakes do a lot of — when they aren't busy biting somebody. I thought I'd see if I could catch it.

"So, I snuck up behind it real slow. I got close to it — it was still just lying there, like it was dead. And I got ready and then reached out and grabbed! the snake behind the head! And you know what?"

"What?"

"That snake wasn't dead. I got my hand right behind its head and then it wrapped its body around my wrist and held on. And that's when I knew I had a problem. Up to then, see, I was in charge. But now, I couldn't let go of the snake until the snake was ready for me to let it go. That put a whole different perspective on things. I'd just have to keep a grip on it until it let me know when it wanted me to let go.

"All the girls thought it was really neat, and I felt pretty cool, walking around with this rattlesnake wrapped around my wrist. Everybody stared and got out of my way. But, really, what can you do with a rattlesnake once you've got it and everybody's seen it? I started to get tired of walking around with it, having to keep a tight grip on it. My fingers were getting tired. I was just praying they wouldn't cramp up. 'Please don't cramp! *Please* don't cramp!' The snake kept trying to fight my grip and wriggle free — those snakes are strong, even little ones like the one I had. I knew I couldn't hold onto it forever.

"Well, finally, after a while — I thought I was going to have to go home with it — the snake let go of my wrist and unwrapped, and I knew that was the sign that he was ready for me to let him go. This was my chance, my big chance, maybe my only chance. But how do you let a rattlesnake go once you've got him in your hand? I didn't know. I finally just figured I'd rear back and give it a toss. So that's what I did. I threw the snake." Fred made a dramatic, full-body motion, as if he were throwing a baseball and his life depended on it.

"I'll tell you one thing, those snakes are fast! Man, they are f-a-s-t! I thought if I threw it hard enough it wouldn't be able to reach back and bite me, but you know, that's exactly what it did. In mid-air it turned around and bit me right on the thumb. See the little scar?"

"Yeah, I do. What happened to the snake?"

"It kept going."

"And then what happened?"

"I went to the hospital. The doctor asked me what happened and I told him. He said, 'That was really dumb.' Then he gave me a shot with a huge needle, right in the butt. Served me right, I guess."

I've also known two others who have been bitten by rattlesnakes, and both were huge men. Todd stood six-foot five in his bare feet.

"You wanna hear about my snakebite, do ya'?" he volunteered. "We were on this fire in the Pacific Northwest. We'd been on it for a while, working way up on this hill, see. It was beautiful country up there, just beautiful. I was glad to be there, that's how beautiful it was.

"I was going back to fire camp on my own, had just done some scouting or something for the crew. I was headed downhill, making good time, and then I had to step over a big log that was in the way. I went like this, see," lifting his leg and demonstrating how a giant steps over a big log. "It wasn't any big deal and then bang!, I really bumped my shin against one of those ol' jagged branches, you know, the ones that stick out of those big logs? Really smacked it a good one. But I kept on going and made it back to camp. By then it was starting to hurt a little bit more than it should, so I thought I'd go over to the first aid tent and get some ice to put on it. I told the lady at the first aid tent what happened, and she said, 'Let's take a look.'

'Yeah,' I said, 'I banged it real good on one of

those big ol' branches.'

She took one look at it and said, 'Why don't you just sit down in that chair over there. That wasn't a branch. You were bitten by a rattlesnake!'"

Barney's run-in with a rattlesnake had an even more bizarre twist to it. A pillar of a man, an expert chain saw operator, he was good at telling the story — the hand movements, the facial gestures, the pregnant pauses, the way he bugged his eyes.

"We were on a fire in Arizona," he started. "Central Arizona, somewhere between Payson and Phoenix. Desert. I hate those desert fires. It's always hotter than heck, and no matter how much water you carry you always seem to run out.

"We'd worked all day on this one stretch of line and it got dark, but we kept working until sometime around midnight. We ate our sack lunches and stretched out for a little nap. The fire wasn't doing anything at all.

"I didn't sleep much. I kept having these *really* weird dreams and waking up. A few hours later we got ready to go back to work, only, I must have slept crooked on my neck because it was mighty sore, right back here." He put one of his huge hands slightly behind and below his right ear.

My neck felt sort of strange, so I asked somebody to take a look at it.

'What do you see?' I asked.

'Two puncture marks a couple inches apart and a dried trickle of blood coming out of each one,' he said. 'Barney, looks to me like some big rattlesnake snuck up on you in the middle of the night and bit you on the neck!'"

Barney bugged his eyes. "Good thing it was a dry bite! I think the snake must have liked me."

Sheep Creek Fire

(First year of fire)

Division M

SLEEPING IN the cold grass at the Dixie Dispatch center in Cedar City, Utah, waiting for our plane to arrive, walking across the tarmac with packs slung over our shoulders, we smelled the exhaust from the engines. The small airport was lit up like a Christmas tree in honor of our pre-dawn departure. Landing in Ely, Nevada just in time for a huge, hot breakfast in a local cafe, then trying to sleep on a converted school bus as we bounced down a dirt road toward the fire, piling our packs in the dirt of a scruffy sagebrush flat. Back on the bus with our fire gear. This is how it began.

The Sheep Creek Fire was calling us.

Our bus driver was a long-haired, bearded, stoic

man who tromped heavily on the accelerator. He drove so hard on the dirt road the folks in the back decided to wear their hard hats, with the chinstrap on. They were taking an awful pounding, bouncing around all over the place. One of us near the front asked the driver what he did for a living, and he said he drove a school bus. We finally jolted and squeaked to a stop. Then he popped open the door and hollered, "Watch your step!" We started the long trudge uphill.

Jack was going to be running the chain saw. I was going to swamp. Tall, blue-eyed behind thick prescription glasses, a hard worker, stoop-shouldered even when he wasn't wearing a heavy field pack — that was Jack. He carried a chain saw over his shoulder. I hefted the red plastic Dulmar container filled with gas and oil. We strapped it onto my field pack.

Anticipating a lot of saw work this shift, Jack asked for a second swamper. Vick, twenty-years old, as tall as Jack and heavily freckled, volunteered. We took turns carrying the Dulmar.

A mile of hiking up into the foothills, following the Sheep Creek drainage, put us at the starting place. The fire had passed through the area the day before and was smoking in only a few scattered places, but Overhead wanted a line around this part of the burn anyway, for peace of mind.

Jack fired up the saw. Vick and I dragged the branches out of the way. There was a lot of mountain mahogany growing on the slope, enough to give Jack and the saw a good workout.

After several hours of steady uphill work, our second wind came and went. The rest of the crew labored behind us with their hand-tools in a long, narrow, dusty line. We had worked hard the day before, peeling logs with pulaskis so we could use them to make a rail fence. Four hours of sleep was all we'd had, before we'd been called out at two o'clock in the morning. We hadn't slept on the plane. Sleeping on the bus was out of the question. When we arrived in camp, Overhead had said, "Oh, good, a fresh crew!" Now we weren't feeling very fresh. We hadn't been fresh when we arrived.

We were tired and started making mistakes. I dragged a large limb from the line, stepping backward without looking, and my left boot heel stubbed on a rock. I stumbled back. My right foot wedged between some other rocks, and down I went. My rear end planted on a sharp branch I had just thrown aside. The jagged piece of tree gouged into my extreme lower right "cheek." I scrambled to my feet and could feel a torrent of blood cascading down the back of my leg.

Frantic, I reached back with my right hand and prodded the area while effectively adhering to the strict fireline code, which is to never drop your drawers on the line unless an angry, stinging insect is involved.

No blood, not a drop. What I thought was blood was actually fresh air spilling into the gaping hole in the back of my trousers.

"Gonna have a scar?" Vick asked. He'd seen me go down.

"Probably."

"You don't want me to —"

"No, that's okay. I'm sure it'll be all right."

"A shame, isn't it?, when you get a good scar like that in a place probably nobody'll ever see."

The folks back at fire camp had told us not to pack a lunch, since they would be helicoptering in sack lunches for everybody. We each had grabbed an MRE just in case, and it was a good thing because our lunches didn't show up and neither did the helicopter. Another rumor bites the dust.

Eating an MRE is a solemn time, a time for reflection. It means that somehow you've gotten yourself into a mess big enough to justify eating an MRE, that's what it means.

I dove into my Beef Slices in Barbecue Sauce. It

came with side packets of applesauce, peanut butter with crackers, condiments, dessert, and an inadequate roll of toilet paper. Originally I had chosen a dehydrated Pork Patties MRE with all the trimmings, opened it up and realized — too late! — the full ramifications of the word "dehydrated." I would have to use some precious water to reconstitute the dried pork briquets! Back in camp, when I picked it out from the box of other MRE's, I had only thought that the word "dehydrated" meant it would be that much lighter to carry.

The Pork Patties resembled rough, dust-dry, grayish-brown brake shoe pads. Discretion is the better part of valor. I treated them accordingly. Here goes! They flew well, sailing easily over some nearby trees.

"Pork Patties?" someone asked, catching only a glimpse of the MRE-turned-UFO.

"Yeah."

"If we were near water you could give them a skip. They sink, you know."

Fortunately for me, somebody else on the crew had packed in two MRE's. He gave me his extra Beef Slices in Barbecue Sauce so I wouldn't go hungry. I chewed on the thin morsels, never before having considered chewing to be a cardiovascular exercise, and looked around at what everybody else was eating. The Chicken A La King, Beef Stew, Chicken/Turkey loaf, and Ham Slices looked quite good, and on future fires I subsequently ranked them according to taste in that order. The Chicken A La King was worth trading for, if you didn't mind giving up a granola bar.

On the outside of each plastic-pouched, camouflage-brown MRE — originally designed for the military — is written the name of the main course. I never knew which side-orders were included, but several of the old-timers had it all committed to memory.

"Trade you my Dehydrated Strawberry packet for your Maple Nut Bar," they'd wager, before a rookie like me had even opened the pouch to see what goodies awaited.

The main courses that were regarded with outright suspicion, if not fear, were those which contained, as the package stated in big, bold, black letters, **"Bean Component — not for pre-flight use."** The hamburger patty MRE contained this warning, as did several others I never had the courage to try. The beans tended to give a person a touch of gas, and if that person were to then go up in an unpressurized airplane or helicopter . . . well, I don't need to go into details. Bean Component gastrointestinal bombs.

After lunch, we continued cutting line uphill, the three of us in the saw team working far ahead of the others. The fire was out in this section, but it was blazing and crowning out higher up on the mountain.

"Be neat to be up there, wouldn't it?" the rookie in me asked the veteran Jack, bent over his chain saw.

"Not really," he replied, glancing up at the billowing smoke as he topped off the gas.

Whenever a chain saw burns the last of the fumes in the tank it accelerates like crazy, revving up to full speed. It happens every hour or two of cutting, depending on how hard the saw is being worked. The first time it happened, Jack was stalking yet another tree when the saw started to howl. He wasn't within ten feet of a tree.

"What's Jack doing?" I thought. "Why's he hotdogging?"

Then the saw sputtered, clunked, and went out, and I knew it was out of gas. The silence was of almost religious proportions.

We finally tied in to a scratchline way up the hill and our work was done. Overhead had told us to stop when we reached the scratchline. The rest of the crew caught up. It usually takes at least ten minutes for the folks in the back to catch up with those in the front.

A convict crew was coming up behind us, a fire crew made up entirely of Nevada Department of Corrections inmates. We stepped aside for them. The fellow leading the crew looked pretty tough. He carried the chain saw over his shoulder and wasn't even breathing hard. The Pulaskis behind him were no pushovers, either. Behind them came the Shovels, but they didn't look nearly as fearsome. None of the men smiled. They all had lots of tattoos. Two uniformed guards accompanied the crew, and they looked as if they'd once been inmates. They didn't do any work, and they didn't carry tools, either. All they carried were guns.

Back at fire camp that night, something wonderful happened. Comfortable in our sleeping bags, surrounded by our red packs, field packs, and boots, we looked up into the incredibly clear Nevada night — the stars overpowering in their countless abundance — and then it began to happen. A meteor shower!

Twice a year, in late August and again in late February, the earth passes through a band of cosmic dust left by a comet. It was spectacular.

"Hey, look at the shooting stars!" somebody announced. People started wriggling around in their sleeping bags, poking their heads out.

"Oh, wow!"

"There's another . . . and another!"

"Look at all of them!"

I watched the shooting stars, entranced, and then rolled over and looked at the smoldering mountain several miles distant, watching the flares of the trees as they burned individually, absolutely silent this far away. They looked like hundreds of twinkling candles. Shooting stars and a burning mountain — nature's fireworks! I slept well that night, as I did every night while on the Sheep Creek Fire. Secure. Nature was my teacher, my providor, my friend. Nature was watching out for me. She would take care of me. I was a rookie.

The next morning I took my first-ever helicopter ride. Before any helicopter trip, there's always a briefing from one of the helitack crewmembers. It's standard procedure. This is what he said.

"I'll call out the names of the people on each flight, and you will follow me over there." He pointed to the dusty helipad behind us. "Do not move toward the ship until I tell you. Right now, check to make sure your chinstrap is secure, goggles are on, gloves are on, and that both earplugs are in. Please button the top button of your shirt and fold your collar up. This will protect you in the event of a fire. Make sure that your pant cuffs are below the top of your boots while in the seat, for the same reason."

He glanced down at his clipboard. "In the event of

a hard landing," (did he mean crash?) "lean forward and wrap your arms under your knees. This position takes most of the pressure off your spine." He looked around at us, making good eye contact, to make sure we were listening. We were.

"As you approach the ship, crouch down and duck to stay clear of the blades. A crewmember there will place your tools and gear in the cargo compartment. Do *exactly* as he says. If something begins to blow away, do not chase it! Tail rotors have killed more than one person, believe me.

"Should you be in a hard landing, (he *did* mean crash!) "do not leave the ship until the rotors have stopped moving. A crewmember will help you with your seatbelt as you board and exit the ship.

"Now, are there any questions?" he asked, wrapping it up. There were none.

"Good. First up we've got . . . "

The whine of the engines kicking in made conversation difficult after that. I didn't want to talk anyway. I just wanted to savor the moment, this excitement — I was going to fly in a helicopter! Man, first they fly us to Nevada, they feed us MRE's, we work with criminals, we get to fly in a helicopter. This is great! And I'm making a lot of money, too!

We were seated inside. The rotors started to kick up, a whole lot of dust and then we lifted off. I was riding in a helicopter! Smiling, confident, I gave Jack a cool thumbs up, even though I really didn't know what I was doing. He had been on a helitack crew the year before, and knew what most of the little dials were for.

The helicopter shook and vibrated more than I was expecting, and seemed altogether quite unstable. It was loud as hell, too, like sitting inside a giant, airborne typewriter, with somebody typing to beat a deadline.

The higher we went, the more we could see of our handline. Then we passed over some slurry patches — long, pink strips in the grass. They looked so funny! The fire had out-flanked the slurry and gone around. There was continuous gray ash everywhere, except in the bright pink patches. Grass poking up through the dried slurry gave it an even more comical air.

I could well imagine the slurry bomber pilot lining up and putting down a beautiful strip of slurry, right in front of the advancing flames — a perfect drop! — pulling out just in time to look over his shoulder and watch the flames pass around the slurry and merrily continue on their way without even slowing down. The pilot would make another run at the fire, of course — his ego getting involved in this next drop — taking his time putting down another beautiful strip.

"Ha!, I've got you this time!" only to have the same thing happen again. And again, and again, until he was out of slurry and had to head back, shaking his fist at the fire.

Sometimes I wonder if they're still there, those funny-looking pink patches of slurry he painted across the Nevada desert.

Guernsey Fire?

(Second year of fire)

Division N

IT WAS not a good fire.

And yes, there *is* such a thing as a good fire. A good fire means lots of overtime and hazard pay, good meals, hot showers at least every third day, a level place to sleep, no injuries or illness, a good crew, occuring in a distant and exotic locale.

A bad fire means just the opposite: normal wages, subsistence meals, no showers, roots and rocks in the sleeping area, a bustling first aid tent, grumpy companions, some place close to home.

It was a bad fire. It had all the makings of a bad fire from the very beginning.

Brett, Margarett, and I were getting sent to a fire on the Arizona Strip in our Model 20 engine. Ricky, the

normal crewmember on our engine, couldn't partici-
pate for one reason or another, so Margarett, a gentle
girl with long blond hair, was asked to fill in.

I had never been to the Arizona Strip before. Never
really had a burning desire to visit, either. People who
lived on the Strip drove like mad, and then took their
time getting out of their pickup trucks.

For those unfamiliar with the Arizona Strip, it's the
geographically isolated expanse of land in the extreme
northwestern section of the state, cut off from the rest
of Arizona by the Grand Canyon. It's smack dab
between the sin of Las Vegas and the moral purity of
Mormon Utah; the beauty and majesty of one of the
seven natural wonders of the world at one end and the
nuclear no-man's land of the Nevada Test Site at the
other.

The Arizona Strip is a place where — rumor has it
— at least one remote community still practices
polygamy. Uranium mines are found here and there.
Ore trucks rumble through town trailing a wake of
geiger counter dust.

Millions of acres of trackless high desert were out
there waiting for us. Our mission: to save some desert
tortoises.

"Tortoises?" we chorused. *"Tortoises!* You've got to
be kidding! Desert tortoises? We're going out in the

middle of nowhere to save a bunch of tortoises?"

"That's what they said."

"Who's they?"

"The folks in charge of the fire. And desert tortoises are endangered. That's why they want you."

Margarett cut in on the conversation. She was a wildlife biologist. "Seems to me the tortoises would just crawl down into their burrows. After all, their species has been around a lot longer than firefighters."

Indeed. Well, whatever the reasons for our foray into the Arizona Strip, we were at least going with our engine, and that was certainly good news. Engines mean soft seats and on-demand air conditioning. AM/FM. Six-packs of soda. Engines will get you out of trouble at sixty miles an hour. And best of all, no engine has ever been dropped off in the middle of nowhere with a crew of other engines and told, "A truck will probably pick you up on the other side of that mountain tomorrow at noon, after you cut line up this side and down the other."

I liked engines. About the only risk was losing your keys and getting locked out.

The three of us headed out of town in our engine, with all the heady confidence that comes from having two full tanks of gas, 200 gallons of water sloshing around in the back, and a ten-year old photocopied map of the Arizona Strip. I tried not to think about the other engine.

The other Model 20 engine, a few years back. People in the district office still liked to tell the story, about how that engine had set out in high spirits, headed for a fire on the Arizona Strip, with two full tanks of gas, a load of water, and an old map.

And about how they'd gotten the vehicle stuck in the middle of nowhere and had to ditch a lot of weight in order to jack themselves out, emptying their 200 gallons onto the Arizona Strip — giving it more water than it had seen in a long time. And pretty soon they were very lost because the old map was no good. Their radio ran on a different frequency than the head office, so they couldn't communicate with anybody. It was hotter than blue blazes and they were running low on gas — and they hadn't seen anybody since leaving town in such high spirits.

Then a rancher in a pickup truck drove by at a high rate of speed and they managed to flag him down, and he stopped but didn't seem to want to get out. And he gave them some gas and drew them a new map on the back of the no-good old map, and they'd finally made it to the head office and told them the fire was out and they were going home.

We took the blacktop all the way and arrived in town. Everybody at the warehouse was busy loading green army cots into a pickup. We helped for a while and then headed into the Strip. The pavement turned to dirt just out of town.

Three hours later we arrived at the fire — what was left of it. The only thing out there was dry grass, prickly pear cactus, yucca, and an occasional juniper to break the monotony. Rolling hills and endless flats and more rocks than necessary stretched all the way to the mountains on the horizon. The ground was black. The fire had apparently come and gone. Where was it now? There wasn't any smoke or anything. Even though I was still relatively new to this business, I did know that if this was a fire then there had to be smoke. It's one of the basic tenants of firefighting.

"Where's the fire, anyway, the part that's still burning?" asked Brett, getting out of the truck. He slammed the door hard and surveyed the wide-open countryside.

"We're not really sure," replied one of the Overhead. "We've got a chopper coming in later so we'll be able to fly it and find out."

Uh-oh. Was this a Guernsey Fire? I'd heard a lot about them, but had never been on one before. They call them Guernsey Fires because Overhead milks them for everything they can. Helicopter rides. Overtime and hazard pay; new tools and supplies, new chain saws and pumps to replace the ones that got broken down or "burned up in the fire." Bring in lots of people and equipment, run up a big tab, and justify a bigger firefighting budget next year.

In fire school the year before, we'd learned about something called the Fire Triangle: heat, fuel, and oxygen. Remove any one of these three elements and fire will not exist. At a Guernsey Fire, there was something jokingly referred to as the Fire Quadrangle: heat, fuel, oxygen . . . and Overhead.

Brett, Margarett, and I set up camp around the engine, disgusted. It looked as if this was going to be home for a while. They both shagged a cot. I preferred sleeping on the ground.

A late-afternoon breeze kicked up and we started to see several thin columns of smoke, far away, way out of smelling distance. Four other crews and half a dozen engines were in camp, plus a first aid tent and the food caterer's truck. I couldn't imagine how the caterers had gotten their truck out here

The sun set, and dinner was served. People made their way through the serving line, holding flimsy paper plates out in front and looking hungry, plunking down at wobbly tables and chairs scattered among the grass and brittlebrush. I got my food and dug in, watching everybody go back for seconds or even thirds. By the time I was done eating, the area was almost deserted. One of the servers walked past, headed for the condiment table. Several yards shy of the table she suddenly stopped short and peered down at the ground. She bent over to get a closer look, cautious.

She jumped back!

"Rattlesnake!" she shouted. "There's a big rattlesnake!" A hundred people had just filed past it at least once, and probably two or three times if they had been really hungry.

"It's *huge!*" She dashed over to one of the trailers, returning with a shiny, new, full-length 2x4. No fire camp is complete without 2x4's. There have to be 2x4's. She advanced toward the snake, the lumber leading the way.

This was quite a woman. She stalked the snake, got within striking distance — exactly eight feet — wound up, and took a swing at the snake that made the earth shudder. No screams, no curses, just, thunk!..thunk-thunk..thunk! and one more — thunk! — to make sure it was dead, which it was, very. The poor snake never had a chance. The woman scooped it up and held it aloft at the end of the beam like a war trophy. She carried it out of camp, limp, and deposited it far on the other side of the trash cans.

The next morning, somebody in Overhead woke up, heard something crawling around in his boot, and at arm's length gingerly poured out another small rattler.

The night itself was also far from dull. The wind picked up at midnight and the blue plastic tarp over our sleeping area billowed and flapped so loudly it woke us all up. I didn't know why we put the darned thing up anyway. Everybody knows it almost never rains on the Arizona Strip. I went back to sleep.

At 1:30 a.m. I woke up again. Something was going on in camp. People were hurrying around and making a racket. I sat up in my sleeping bag. Margarett was just waking up. Brett was lacing his boots.

"What's going on?"

"Fire's coming! Getting ready to move camp! Overhead says it's almost got us surrounded!"

I scrambled out of my sleeping bag, put my boots on. The tarp came down next. With lightning speed, we packed everything and made ready to leave — pronto!

Then it started to rain.

Brett and I scrambled to put up the tarp. The rain put out the wildfire and fire camp turned muddy. We went back to sleep, even more disgusted than before.

At dawn we woke up.

"Eric, could you come over here? My leg hurts." Margarett was sitting on her cot.

"Sure. What's up?"

"I don't know. My knee hurts." Her voice had a slight tremor to it.

I went over. "Maybe you banged it yesterday against the dashboard or the gearshift on the way in. That road was terrible."

"No, I don't think so. It feels like something bit me on the back of my knee. Could you see if you see anything?"

There was a small red spot on the back of her knee, a mark about the size of a nickel. "You're right." I tried not to make her worry. "It doesn't look very bad, though."

"It sure does hurt."

Several minutes later, she called me again. "Eric, my foot's starting to hurt, too." Her knee and foot weren't swollen at all, just that little red mark on the back of her knee.

A minute later, "Ooh, my hip hurts, too." Something strange was going on. I told her to sit tight, and then I jogged over to get Brett. He was meeting with Overhead. They wanted us to mop-up the fire's soggy east flank with the water from our engine. I told him about Margarett. We hurried back to check on her.

"My other leg hurts, too. It really hurts." She tried to walk but was stiff, awkward. We helped her to the first aid tent. Overhead was there, too.

"What happened?"

"We think something bit her on the back of her right knee. It spread pretty fast down her leg, and now her other leg's starting to hurt."

"Is she on your engine?"

"Yeah." Brett was doing all of our talking.

First Aid talked it over with Overhead. Something bad was happening to Margarett, the gentle girl with the long blond hair.

"Okay." Overhead reached a decision. "Why don't the three of you get in your engine and take her to the hospital."

"Oooh, both my hips hurt, and my stomach's starting to feel strange."

"That's a three-hour drive," Brett noted.

"You'll be there by ten o'clock. I'll radio ahead and tell them you're on your way."

"Brett, my legs really do hurt."

"I know." He turned to Overhead. "Listen, something's happening to her. You still have that helicopter here?"

"Sure do. We'll be going up in a little bit to scout the fire."

"My stomach hurts." Her legs were starting to tremble.

"I think you should fly her to the hospital." It was one of the best decisions Brett ever made in his life.

"Well —" Overhead looked at Margarett. She was sniffling, starting to cry, not like her at all. "Okay. I'll get the pilot and she'll be on her way."

"Brett, my hands are starting to hurt, too. What's happening to me?"

"Hurry!"

They flew full speed to the hospital and arrived just in time. Margarett's breathing was coming short and she couldn't move her arms and legs by the time they landed. She'd been bitten by a black widow spider on the back of her knee and had a severe allergic reaction to the poison. Black widow spiders aren't native to that part of the Arizona Strip. It had come from the warehouse and crawled out of her cot.

She was still in intensive care when we were

demobilized from the fire and sent home. Five days there and we'd never even seen the fire! We stopped in at the hospital to see her. Margarett was propped up in bed, and had trouble moving her arms and legs. She would be out of action for most of the summer.

Brett and I both knew if we'd taken her to the hospital in our engine — three hours of rough and rocky dirt road — dear sweet Margarett probably would have died before we got halfway there, somewhere out in the middle of the Arizona Strip. Good thing they had the helicopter.

Oak Grove Fire

(Second year of fire)

Division O

It was 2:30 in the morning and somebody was knocking hard on my door. I pulled back the curtain to look. It was Brett.

"They want you to go on that fire!"

"Okay. Are you going, too?"

He looked at me strangely. "Of course I'm going."

The long, washboarded drive into town was a quiet one. I was driving.

"How are you feeling, anyway?" I asked

He gave me another strange look. "'How are you feeling?' What's that supposed to mean? How do I look?"

I thought he looked like hell. Not even three hours

ago, almost the entire seasonal staff on the district —
firefighters, timber cruisers, and wildlife assistants —
had been engaged in a heavyweight, "Who me,
worry?" drinking spree. It was tradition, the monthly
full moon party at our lookout tower. Everybody who
showed up took turns climbing up the tower. They'd
given a thrilling play-by-play account of the Oak
Grove Fire.

"Boy, it's really going now! Glug, glug, glug.

"You can see the flames from here!" Glug.

"Bet ya' a six-pack we get sent out on that tomorrow!" Glug, glug.

Meeting at the district office at sunrise, you could
immediately tell who had made the long journey to
and from the lookout tower the night before just by
looking at them. They were drinking coffee by the
cupful and gathering near the water fountain. The victims of the full moon talked in hushed tones and practically tiptoed in their heavy leather work boots. I was
amazed that some of them had made it this far.

Ask any one of them at that moment if there was
one thing in his life that he would like to go back and
change, and I think to a man they would have meekly
replied, penitant, whispering, "I wouldn't have gone
out drinking last night."

But it was too late now. I knew it, they certainly knew it. We were headed for the Oak Grove Fire. Here we come, ready or not.

We were hoping for heavy timber for miles in all directions, cool, lush meadows with lots of wildflowers waving in the breeze, streams that happily gurgled their way through rolling hills, watering shady glades.

But it wasn't like that at all where we were going, not at the Oak Grove Fire. Where the fire was, the country was hot, hot, hot. Hot, dry, and dusty. And bright! Man, it was *bright*.

It was the worst kind of stuff to fight fires in, too. Thick, continuous clusters of chaparral and scrub oak, too thick to crawl under and too tall to see over; the only way was to thrash and chop your way through the mess. The bushes had a dusty coating that shook off when you took a good whack. It made you sneeze, hard. Fire moved fast and burned loud and hot through this kind of stuff. Poison ivy smoke hurt your lungs. Be on the lookout for rattlesnakes. Don't get dehydrated. This was no fun. And we hadn't even started to work yet.

Freddy, our reluctant crew boss, organized us by squads. Everybody had been hanging out in the shade with their sunglasses on. The full-mooners, taking very short steps, started trudging up the hill.

Not even an hour out of the dirt parking lot, one of the rookies on the crew, a grim semi-survivor of the lookout tower blowout, noticed me taking a sip of water from one of my canteens.

"Can I have some of your water?" he asked. He looked so awful that I said sure — as long as he didn't touch it with his lips. He did anyway.

"Finish it up, then," I said, and he did, too, right there on the spot, the whole quart right down the hatch. Glug, glug, glug.

I lasted almost an hour longer.

Oh, sure, I could have gone on, if I hadn't had to go to the hospital.

What happened was this. We'd only gone half a mile up the line, pushing our way through the brush and clearing a path as we went. The fire made a good run. It stayed well away from us, but got us to thinking about locating a really good safety zone. Several fellows on the crew were sent off in search, and returned with a good report. They'd found a big, beautiful rockfield up ahead.

Freddy wanted all of us to see where it was, just in case. We'd take a quick look at it and then some of us would come back to finish the stretch of line. The others would keep working farther ahead.

We examined the rockfield from a distance. It looked adequate, certainly, but seemed a little too far away for my preference. That's the thing about safety zones — they're especially nice if you can get to them in a hurry. Freddy decided to call Overhead on the radio and talk to them about the safety zone situation. The fire was still cooking right along. We could hear it scorching through the brush. Chaparral and scrub oak are really nasty when they burn. The fire sent up a thick, yellowish-black column. Freddy was having trouble with the battery on his radio.

"Eric, could you get a new one from my pack?"

"Sure." He handed me the old battery.

"Put it in the top pocket. The good ones are in the bottom pocket."

"You bet." I retrieved a fresh battery and handed it to him. He took it.

"Thanks."

And that's when it happened. Thunk. Something hit my right foot. I looked down. Freddy's pulaski was lying in the dirt at my feet. My boot had a four-inch slash in it. Blood was trickling through the gap. Dang! Freddy had been leaning on his pulaski, business end up, and when he moved his arm to take the battery the axe blade had dropped down into my foot. It was the end of the Oak Grove Fire for me and I knew it. It hurt. And those were my favorite boots.

"Sorry about that, guy," he said, swiping at my hard hat with his glove. I could tell he felt badly.

"If only you'd done more work with your pulaski, Freddy, it wouldn't have been so sharp!" somebody joked. I sat down and peered through the slash in my boot. There was a cut on the end of my little toe. It wasn't too bad, but it sure was bleeding.

"Gonna need a few stitches in that for sure," someone else announced, kneeling down to look at it.

"Why don't you get on back to the parking lot and they'll get you all set up." I went on my way, hobbling down the line, carrying my shovel, trying to keep my boot out of the dirt.

Not more than an hour later I was in the passenger seat of a Forest Service rig, heading into town with my foot sticking out the window. There had been accident forms to do in triplicate before they'd release me to see the doctor. That's one of the standard jokes about the Forest Service: once you see how much paperwork there is to fill out, you won't want to have any more injuries.

The driver turned on the radio, and we listened to the local station. The disc jockey cut in for a news bulletin.

"And this just in . . . there's been a firefighter injured on that forest fire near town. He was struck by an axe and is being rushed to the hospital. No other details are available at this time."

I waved out the window at the people in the other cars, but they gave me funny looks. I pointed at my foot, but it didn't help.

"Hey, that's me!"

Limping into his office the next day, I met with one of the district officials. Whenever a person has an accident or gets hurt, he or she has to sit down and have a chat with one of the head honchos. It's yet another intimidation device to discourage accidents and injuries, probably more effective than paperwork in triplicate. One of our district's fire officers was there, too. He'd been up in Salt Lake City the day before and had heard on the television news about a firefighter getting struck by an axe and being rushed to the hospital.

I told them both what had happened.

"*Freddy* did this?" the district official asked, incredulous. "Your crew boss? *Our* Freddy?" Crew bosses weren't supposed to do that sort of thing.

"Two stitches on your little toe, that's it? That's all that happened?" the fire officer asked, interested.

"That's all. A hundred and eighty dollars worth."

"We'll just take that out of Freddy's next paycheck," mumbled the district official, joking, though I had the feeling he would have if he could have.

The fire officer was intrigued. "The way they were talking about you on the TV news, they made it sound as if you were lucky to be alive. There's even something about it in today's paper."

"Really?"

"Yeah. You're famous."

But the district official was still shaking his head. "Golly, *golly!* Isn't this something, though?" he said, smacking the table with the flat of his hand. "We send out a bunch of drunks on a fire, and one of the only sober guys on the crew gets a pulaski stuck in his foot!"

Kelsey Fire
(Third year of fire)

Division P

It was late August.

We were going to California.

I had never been firefighting there. Firefighters consider California to be the promised land of wildland fire, a sort of mecca. A Bermuda Triangle. The last several years it hadn't burned much, but this year it was burning right on schedule. When California burns, it usually gets going sometime in August.

Dry lightning the week before had ignited 2,000 forest fires in northern California and southern Oregon. Eight hundred crews — 16,000 people! — the entire firefighting might of the U.S. Forest Service, National Park Service, and Bureau of Land Management, plus state, county, and volunteer fire departments — everybody was going to California.

I watched the C-141 taxi in. It looked sinister, with camouflage green and black paint, no passenger windows, and a nose like a shark's mouth.

We lined up single file, carrying a red pack over one shoulder and initial attack gear over the other. The gangway in the back came down and we walked up into the cavernous bay. The jet engines were on idle; the pilot hadn't even bothered to shut them down. We lined up on the sides, deposited our gear in a huge pile on the cargo ramp, and took our places on the webbing seats. Half of us faced the other half, forty people in each row. We put on our seatbelts. It would be a four-hour flight to Redding. One of the crewmen gave a pre-flight safety briefing. The engines took hold.

I was seventh from the front on the left side as we walked in from the back. With the plane taxiing across the tarmac, the fellow at the very back end of my row raised his hand. He spoke to the crew member back there. Something was wrong. A voice came over the loudspeaker.

"The guy at the back end on the left side of the plane doesn't have a seatbelt. I want everybody on that side of the plane to look behind you and see if you have an extra set of seatbelts."

The fellow two seats up from me, in seat number five, raised his hand. "I do!" shouting loudly above the noise of the engines.

The loudspeaker clicked on. "Okay. Now everybody in that row, after the fellow raising his hand near the front, I want each of you to take off your seatbelt and give it to the person on your right! Repeat, give your seatbelt to the person on your right!" Thirty-some of us took off our seatbelts in unison, like we'd somehow practiced the maneuver, slid forward in the webbing seats (it was very awkward), and passed the seatbelt behind us to the person on our right. It looked good up to that point, but then things rapidly fell into disorder, even chaos.

People up and down the row yelled above the shrill whine of the engines.

"Is this my belt? Did you just give me this one now, or was it the one I already had on?"

"I don't know, they all look the same!"

"I got this one, but I don't know whose it is!"

"I think it's mine!"

"The one from before, or the one you're supposed to have?"

"I don't know, maybe it's yours!"

"Are you sure?"

"Yes, I think so!"

"Does it look like yours?"

"Which one?"

"You!"

"No, I mean which seatbelt!"

"The one before or after?"

Loudspeaker came on again. "Does everybody have a seatbelt?" giving the impression that it really didn't matter whether we had a seatbelt or not; we were taking off and that's just the way it was going to be. The engines revved up. The plane accelerated down the runway with a roar and took off at a steep angle, pushing us sideways in our seats. Four hours and we'd be in Redding.

After what seemed like the longest four hours of our lives — cramped, noisy, and a little cold — the plane began its descent into Redding.

Loudspeaker: "My partner in the rear of the airplane can't find his sunglasses! Please look for them behind you and under your seat!" Behind and under the webbing seats were loose bundles of extra webbing, assorted ropes, and straps of all colors. It was a real mess. We diligently poked through the clutter but found nothing.

We shook our heads. Negative. There was a

moment of silence, except for the engines.

"Please look again for my partner's sunglasses!" So we dutifully looked and again found nothing; another short silence, then Loudspeaker, beginning to sound angry.

"Nobody leaves this place until those sunglasses are found!" We couldn't believe it, what a bozo! A minute later his temper, definitely came through.

"I mean it, nobody leaves this plane until those sunglasses are turned in!" Several people on the starboard side opposite me began discreetly flipping off Loudspeaker. The fellow beside me leaned over and said, "Next thing you know he'll say they won't land the plane until the glasses turn up."

In spite of Loudspeaker, the landing gear went down with a thump. It was a good landing. The back ramp went down, and we filed off in long, twin rows. Welcome to California.

The air in Redding smelled smoky-sweet, and the sunrise was tinted reddish-grey. A friend of mine, a firefighter who'd been on a fire in California for three weeks, not far from where we eventually ended up, once told me, "Man, it was weird over there in northern California. Three weeks on the line. I felt like I lost a piece of my brain over there."

We stepped into a shiny clean touring bus — impressed — and headed north, pulling in to eat at a cafeteria-style restaurant on the edge of town. It was all-you-can-eat, and I believe they lost money on us, eating our first real food in two days. I personally made up for lost time with the salad, pasta, and rolls; food like that is usually in short supply in fire camp. Meat and potatoes — there would be plenty of that in camp, there always is. So I ate a good lunch, a good lunch to travel on, and slept a little on the bus ride, lulled to sleep by the belches from the guys who had eaten one-too-many chicken-fried steaks.

Three hours later we pulled into Yreka, pronounced "Wy-reeka" not "Eureka!" We got out, lounged in the grass for a while, then were moved to a ranger station at Scott River. Only the crew bosses got off the bus this time. We must be getting close. The closer you are to the fire, the harder it is to get information. When they returned they gave us the lowdown.

We were to drive down the road to another Forest Service duty station, have dinner, and spend the night there. The next day we would drive about 25 miles farther west to the Kelsey Creek Ranger Station, our final destination. They directed us to the temporary staging area, a Forest Service maintenance yard with a cow pasture out back, where we'd spend the night.

Unfortunately, the dirt driveway leading into the maintenance yard was too narrow for our big touring bus. I was sitting at a window toward the back, on the right side facing the front. We'd almost completed the sharp turn when an awful, metal-on-metal tearing sound suddenly came from the wheelwell directly below me. My pal Jerry, sitting at the aisle, said, "What the — !" Our beautiful bus ground to a painful halt.

The driver jumped out, jogged around to the back, and cut loose with a fantastic string of expletives. I could hear him through the closed window. Even if I hadn't been able to hear him, I could easily have read his lips. He'd snagged the tire on a fire hydrant near the mailbox.

Our bus limped into the dirt parking lot and stopped. We hurried off and grabbed our gear from the luggage compartment, commenting about how difficult it must be to change the rear tire on a touring bus. Walking through a scattering of wood buildings, we could smell charcoal burning. The woman tending the grill yelled, "How do you like your steaks?" A little further on, we got our first look at the grassy pasture. All the cows were gone. This was going to be just fine.

Ever since we'd left Yreka, forest fire smoke had

become increasingly heavy. It blotted out the afternoon sunshine and made every vehicle on the road —
cars, motorcycles, and fire trucks — drive with their
headlights on. I wondered what we were were getting
into.

Jerry and I found a level place to put down our
ground tarp and spread out our government-issue
sleeping bags. We always did that first thing; it let the
bags air out and regain their loft. Then we walked over
to help set up for dinner and do some scouting, see
what was good to eat, then wash up before the meal.
But there wasn't much to do, so we went to see how
the driver was coming along with the tire. He didn't
need our help.

We went back to the crew. Everybody was sitting
around, talking, a few playing cards. Nothing going on
there, either. We lined up and headed over to the
chow line when our crew boss, Jim, came back. He
said the bus tire was coming along okay, but the driver
seemed a little cranky.

We sat down at the long tables, wobbly since they
were out on the grass. The woman had done a really
nice job with the steaks. Still hungry I got up for a
banana and came back to find several black specks
floating in my milk and sprinkled over the salad, looking like big, black, pepper flakes. What was this? I

hoped nobody had spiked my food while I was gone.

I looked around. Jerry . . . ? Nobody looked too guilty. There were little black specks all over the table. Where had they come from? They weren't there when I'd gotten up for the banana.

I looked up. Little black specks were falling all around us, like the first snow of the season. Black snow. Ash; ash from those 2,000 forest fires. The ash started to come down even heavier.

"Jerry, do you —"

"Yeah, I see it. What's going on, man? I hope it's not what I think it is."

Several minutes later, the ash came down in flurries. Mixed in with it were larger pieces of charred pine needles and burnt pieces of bark. This was fascinating. I'd never heard of anything like this before. It was like being downwind of a volcanic eruption. We could see countless pieces slowly swirling down, hundreds and hundreds of them, up to an inch long. I reached for my cup of milk and had to skim the floating pieces off the top.

Curious — and more than a little concerned — we turned to one of the fellows who worked on the district.

"Where's the nearest fire, anyway?"

I remember his exact words.

"As near as we can tell, the closest major fire is about twenty miles west of here, near Kelsey Creek."

Twenty miles! Oh my God! If this fire is strong enough to rip needles and bark off the trees and hurl them so high that they can fall twenty miles away, well, we've got a major problem here. None of us said anything in reply. *Twenty miles* — was that possible?

For several minutes we chewed in silence, each of us thinking to ourselves what a real mess we had gotten ourselves into this time. Jerry was sitting across from me. Our moment of silence over, he leaned toward me and said, "We are going to be here for a long, *long* time."

The dinner didn't taste nearly as good after that, and I only went up for one more helping of potatoes. It looked as if they'd been heavy with the pepper. Ash. They put the lid on.

Division Q

WE WOKE up the next morning at six. All of our gear was covered with a layer of ash.

After breakfast we organized our things and climbed on the bus. It had a new tire. The driver took his time clearing the driveway. Our next stop was going to be Kelsey Fire camp, deep in the heart of the Klamath Mountains.

The drive was slow and winding, passing cow pastures and summer homes as we headed into the foothills. All of the houses looked eerily deserted and lifeless, cloaked in an other-worldly wrapping of gray smoke. This was getting weird. Few people would ever witness anything like this. Conversation was sporadic. Everybody was too busy trying to make sense of it all. We were headed into the unknown.

We drove for an hour, going slowly on account of the poor visibility. Several times we passed full logging trucks coming from deep in the mountains. Logging trucks? Here the whole world was burning up and they were still logging? I couldn't believe it! Yeah, I know, these loggers had house payments and car repair bills, their kids needed braces, somebody's birthday was probably coming up; yeah, I can accept that. But this, this was different. Couldn't they understand that it was no longer business as usual. Couldn't they see what was happening here?

The road entered the mountains and was swallowed by the smoke, the trees, and the curves. We kept going, slower. The bus struggled up a hill, and turned off the main road. We very carefully hung a sharp right turn between several towering ponderosa pine trees, and then pulled into a big grassy opening. Kelsey Fire camp.

We got off, once more grabbed our gear, and headed over to a distant part of the clearing. It looked secluded and quiet over there. We bedded down under some trees, in a little fenced-off enclosure. It was really nice: grassy and almost flat. There was a nearby outhouse, and beside it a cabin with a massive, brass padlock on the door. Good thing it wasn't the other way around. There was a water spigot outside the house, so we could fill our canteens. All we needed was food. We were the first crew to arrive in camp. Within a week there would be crews from Pennsylvania, Kentucky, Montana, Texas, and Alaska, to name just a few of the states represented.

Fire camp is actually a lot like civilization. I had taken an anthropology class in college about it and learned that civilizations often go through several distinct stages: formation, rise to power and prestige, post-glory decline, and then, finally, decay and abandonment. Most of the time Kelsey Fire camp looked as if it were in the throes of decay and abandonment.

We lined up and headed over to dinner when Overhead came to get us.

In spite of the fact that we hadn't done any real physical activity for the past two full days except eat, we were looking forward to dinner. We always did, whether we were hungry or not. It was a time to unwind, relax, laugh, and eat as much as our bodies could hold. Slowly walking single file past the trays of chicken, canned corn, mashed potatoes, and bread, holding out our paper plates and trying to keep them from spilling, we usually made it a habit to say hello to the servers and strike up a short conversation, hoping to make both our day and theirs a little nicer. Many times on other fires, the servers — kind, matronly women — would ask where our crew was from. We'd tell them, and in reply they would say that they had a cousin, or a friend of a friend who lived near there. Then it was time to move on and ask for gravy on the mashed potatoes, please.

This first night, however, the food servers were all young men in their mid-to-late 20's, wearing matching faded denim jackets and jeans. They seemed nice enough, and I thought they were probably from a nearby town, probably from a civic group or something like that, helping out like the locals often do when the mountain behind their town is on fire.

So I said hello to this one fellow, manning the tray of fried chicken. He looked a lot like me; about 25 years old, 5'10", blond hair, clean cut. I asked him where he was from.

"Bakersfield area," he replied.

Thinking about how nice it must be to be up in the cool pines at Kelsey, I asked, "Does it feel good to be out?" But just as I was saying that — the tail end of the words just leaving my mouth, crossing the final "t" — a thought flashed through my mind.

"Hey, this guy might be from one of those convict labor details!" Sometimes they're assigned to help out on big fires. He was! Too late! The words were on display and I almost tripped over myself adding, "Out!- I mean, er, out of the heat and up into the cool high country?"

He stared at me coldly and gave me a wing and a scrawny drumstick, not saying a word. His glare said everything he wanted it to say, something between, "I cannot believe you just said that!" and, "You son of a bitch."

I hastily moved on to the next server, also young, wearing blue denim, only this time all I said was "Thanks," heading for a distant table. Jerry made sure that everyone at our table heard the story. They were generous with it, and told it to everybody else.

Another light dusting of ash fell during dinner.

After the meal, Jerry and I filled our canteens and stuffed some oranges and granola bars into our field packs. Then I put fresh batteries into my headlamp and set out a clean pair of socks. Gloves went in the pocket of my field pack, so I wouldn't lose them in the morning; hard hat went on top. I was ready to go out on the fireline. Fire ready!

Slowly, thoroughly, I brushed my teeth. Taking good care of your teeth is one of the few luxuries available to firefighters in fire camp. Everything else that happens to you is almost totally beyond your control: when and what you eat, if/when you get to shower, how much work you do and what you carry, when you sleep, when you wake, when you go home. Everything is decided by somebody else. To have even one totally personal, controllable, beneficial activity at your disposal, even something as simple as brushing your teeth, is a real blessing. To go to sleep with squeaky-clean teeth was a small bit of sanity in an otherwise controlled and often crazy existence. I flossed, too.

It was interesting to see what other people did to keep their sanity intact in northern California. Each person approached things from a slightly different angle. Jerry lived for a piping hot mug of tea every morning. He'd lace up his boots with a flourish and head over to the hot drink section near the food serving line first thing, making a beeline for the tall caldrons of hot water and the box of tea bags. He always looked so calm, at peace over there, slowly dunking a tea bag into his steaming cup of water. That was his escape; the fireline was a million miles away.

I drank a lot of hot chocolate — it was cold up in the mountains, with fall colors just starting to arrive — but never with the perseverence, the focus, the dogged intensity with which Jerry pursued his morning cup of tea. The world could have come to a crashing halt and it wouldn't have mattered, as long as he had his tea.

Some people regularly stretched before and after the shift, like athletes limbering up at a big event. Others escaped into books they toted in their red packs, finding that reading even two or three pages at the end of the day by the light of a headlamp cleared their minds, and relaxed them enough for sleep. I always got a kick out of watching them work their way across and down the page — wearing their hard hats the whole time — turning their heads when they turned each page. If you asked them what they were reading they'd look up at you and accidentally flash you with the light.

"Is your book any good?"

"Yeah, it sure is," and the light went up and down.

Division R

THE NEXT morning somebody from Overhead told Jim, our crew boss, the law of the land. Apparently, our very existence depended on our bus.

"That bus is your transportation for the next two weeks!" Overhead warned. "Don't let anybody else get their hands on it or you'll all be walking!" Available transportation was in such short supply, owing to the sudden influx of 16,000 firefighters, that everything was fair game. Old yellow school buses, convict crew trucks, military trucks, even personal vehicles were being used to trundle the firefighters around. I saw more than one very full station wagon go past, riding low in back, shovel handles sticking out the windows.

We lucked out. Our bus was a relatively new

model and was in remarkably good condition, before it did duty on these fires. It had a cassette stereo, tinted windows, and cushioned seats. Talk about traveling in style, man! we had it made! It was even better than riding in a fire engine! It was the only fire dispatch that any of us could remember where we could use the restroom on the way to the fireline.

Our driver was a real character, from Las Vegas, Nevada — the dark side of the Arizona Strip. Said he'd been woken up by a telephone call at 2 a.m. the morning we all got sent out.

"Get a week's worth of gear and be at the bus depot as soon as you can!" he was fond of repeating.

He was firmly attached to his bus, in mind, body, and soul. He slept in it. Every night he would open the luggage compartment and crawl into the long cargo bay. We'd watch him in there rolling out his bedroll, hunched over so he wouldn't bump his head. He'd close the door from the inside but leave it slightly ajar, for air, I guess.

And every morning after breakfast Jim or Alex would go over and knock on the aluminum paneling and wake him up.

"Good morning! We're about ready to go."

"Uh, yeah," his deep morning voice echoed out of the luggage compartment. "*Damn* it got cold last night!"

The door would swing open a minute later and he would step outside, stretch, fetch himself a cup of coffee, get the keys, and away we'd go.

Like a race-car driver, he viewed his fifty-foot vehicle as an extension of his immortal self. But the roads in the Klamath Mountains were primarily designed for logging trucks, and that's where the conflict came. Logging truck drivers, judging by the design and placement of their roads, also tend to view themselves as indestructable.

Two lane or one, smooth or potholed, graded or washboarded, level or climbing, straight or twisted; logging roads all had one thing in common. They weren't made for a greyhound bus.

We knew it. Our driver knew it. Overhead knew it. The bus certainly knew it. But we had no choice. It was either this, or walk. The majestic touring bus was our sole form of transportation.

On one of our first mornings on the Kelsey Fire, we left the security of the blacktop and turned onto a dirt road. Our driver frantically double-clutched in the darkness as the bus struggled up a steep grade. Luminous green lights from the dashboard lit the driver's face and cast a hideous glow. It scared me to stare at him, but I couldn't help it. He looked like a grimacing, unshaven, radioactive version of the Grim Reaper. I couldn't figure out how he managed to drive, gazing through his ghoulish reflection in the flat windshield. We topped out and then made a sharp left turn. The logging road angled down toward a shallow drainage. Or was it shallow?

Our driver stopped the bus at the edge of the dry creekbed, alternating between running both hands through his hair and clenching the steering wheel so hard we could see his knuckles. He leaned forward and peered through the windshield at the wash, wide and studded with big rocks.

He looked up at us in the wide mirror above his head. He could see us and we could see him.

"I don't know about this one," he said, searching for sympathy and understanding. We were in a rowdy mood that morning. One wise guy at the back yelled, "Go for it!" and the rest of us took up the chant, drowning out the words on the radio. The driver stared down at the creekbed and turned on his high beams.

"Go for it!" we hollered. He glanced at us in the mirror, giving us a half-smile that came out a little awkward.

"Go for it!" He looked one last time at the impass and sat back down in his seat, nodding.

"Go for it!" He punched the accelerator. Peer pressure can be an awful thing.

The engine roared like a lion.

The flat nose of the bus plunged downward and entered the wash. The driver punched the gas again, harder. He was committed.

The back tires followed next, and dropped into the creekbed.

It was now or never for both the bus and the driver. He had no choice; hideous metal-on-rock noises came from the chassis and the rear fender of the bus. The driver gave it all he had.

"Pedal to the metal!" we shouted in spontaneous cheer, being real jerks, but it felt good, anyway.

The roar of the engine almost drowned out the horrible screeching coming from the back end of the bus. I hoped nobody was using the restroom. We cringed. Our driver took on the appearance of a ghastly Hunchback of Notre Dame. I wished he'd turn off those dashboard lights.

The bus lurched, struggled magnificently, surged, and suddenly we were free and clear, plowing up the far side as the wheels grasped for traction, engine at full RPM, the driver down-shifting like a madman.

"Nice job!" We let out a cheer, not feeling like jerks any more. It was also a good feeling.

Still clenching his teeth a mile down the road, as thick, overhanging tree branches scratched and scraped against the vehicle's shiny exterior, the driver announced for our benefit, "This bus is worth a quarter of a million dollars! Yeah, that's right, two-hundred and fifty thousand dollars!"

"It's not going to be worth fifty cents by the time we're done with it," the bearded fellow across the aisle from Jerry noted. "It's gonna look like the bus in 'The Gauntlet,' you know, that movie with Clint Eastwood, when he hijacks a bus and the police shoot it full of holes and trash it at the end?"

More than once we would finish our line assignment and gather at a remote drop point — they doubled as pick-up points, too — and as we talked to our division boss or other Overhead, our shiny bus could be heard struggling up a nearby grade. Touring buses make their own special kind of noise. Everybody at the drop point could tell this wasn't one of the standard deuce-and-a-half military transport trucks that almost every other crew was riding around in, now that they'd activated the National Guard.

"What's *that?*"

Our bus could be seen ghosting through the trees, on a dirt track that had not ever seen a passenger car and probably never would. The other firefighters couldn't quite make it out, but it sure did look like a bus.

"What *is* that?"

With our bus coming into full view, Overhead would invariably do a double-take and cry, "Good lord, a greyhound bus! Now I've seen everything!"

"Well, here's our ride," we'd announce, lining up. The bus would make a sweeping turn and stop right in front of us. The door would swing open with an air-pressure hiss.

We were veritable celebrities around fire camp, too. Lots of people thought we must have been some kind of elite firefighting unit to justify the bus.

"I heard you were one of the guys on that crew I saw yesterday, riding around in the bus. If you don't mind me asking, what kind of crew is that, anyway?"

Division S

OUR DAY began at 4:45 a.m. Each squad boss woke everybody in his squad. My squad boss was a nice fellow named Sam. He had an interesting way of waking us. All he did was just give two quick, short whistles between his teeth, sort of like a bird chirping. Many of us slept with earplugs to keep out the racket of the camp's diesel generators, and the noise of night shift leaving for the line. But it didn't matter if we had earplugs or not, we'd still hear Sam and his soft bird whistles. One soft chirp and we were up and at 'em.

Then it was take off the wool cap and the long underwear — it got colder each night — replacing them with fire clothes. The boots went on last. Give the sleeping bag a shake and cover it to keep the ash off. Same routine every morning.

Then off to the hand warmers. These were five-foot tall metal pipe devices that burned a combination of diesel fuel and who-knows what else. We called them "smudge pots" since they gave off so much bluish-gray smoke. Some ingenious soul had swiped several straw bales from the generator area (the bales were stacked around the generators to deafen the noise) and we used these as chairs around our smudge pot. Our whole crew could be seen over there before breakfast as we rounded everybody up. We didn't go to breakfast until everybody was ready.

We usually didn't do much talking around the smudge pots. Gut-wrenching coughs nipped conversation at the bud; steady, hacking coughs, like those of a heavy smoker. Merely breathing the air in the Klamath area was the equivalent of smoking eight to ten packs of cigarettes a day, each and every day — that's how smoky it was. And this didn't include the worse air on the fireline, with the dust and ash kicked up by our tools. The harder we worked, the more of it we breathed. It just didn't seem fair, to happen to such good people. When we cut "hot" line it was even worse, with the fire right there in front of our faces, reflected in our eyes.

Behind our smudge pot was a long row of a dozen or so J-Johns. Contracted out by the federal government, they cost about a hundred dollars per day, per "unit." On any fire you could immediately tell how serious Overhead was taking the fire by the number of outhouses in camp. Flatbeds filled with port-a-potties rolling into camp meant you were staying for a while; one or two privies tucked discreetly behind a tree at the far edge of fire camp meant you would be home in several days. By the end of our first week at Kelsey Fire camp, there were twenty-five J-Johns, maintaining a proper ratio of one outhouse for each twenty-person crew in camp. I hated to see them arrive. Each one that was set up in camp was a testimonial to how long we'd be there, another nail in our coffin, so to speak.

On a more positive note, the colors of the "units" varied, and the casual observer could see practically every color of the rainbow: orange, green, yellow, red, grey, blue. Green was by far the most popular color. They blended in well with the forest surroundings.

"I think I'll go to the green room now."

"I've heard that the lavender room is beautiful this time of the morning, when the sun isn't even up yet."

(A grandmotherly friend of mine who went to a wedding in England said that the septic system at the reception backed up the day before the festivities.

They were expecting a big crowd. They called in a port-a-potty company to solve the problem. The company delivered several units just in time.

"And you know, they were the poshest I'd ever seen!" my friend told me.) No fire camp J-John will ever be described as "posh," and I will leave it at that.

Our life of luxury and decadence came to an end on day ten.

Jim was especially grim that morning. We could always tell what sort of day awaited us when he returned from his post-breakfast meeting with Overhead. If he seemed happy and smiled, then we'd probably be back for dinner at a reasonable hour. A set, determined look to his face meant we had a long day ahead of us.

"Better get an extra granola bar on the way out of camp." We hated to hear him say that.

But that morning, well, the mere posture of Jim, the way he dragged himself away from Overhead, this could be the bad news to end all bad news. It almost made you cry just looking at him.

"Sorry to tell you this, gang, but I'm afraid we won't be seeing any more of our bus." He sighed from the bottom of his heart. "From here on out, we'll be taking a deuce."

We lined up single file, our morale somewhere down near our boot heels. Rarely has there been a more stoic and solemn procession in the proud tradition of firefighting in the U.S. Forest Service than when we said goodby to our bus.

In it's place, a deuce-and-a-half — we called them "deuces" — an open-air, military transport truck. They seat twenty people, a full crew in the back and room for no more.

These deuces were Korean War remnants, 1953 vintage, older than some Overhead. They could burn any fuel except refried beans. Ours was driven by a young, wet-behind-the-ears National Guardsman; he seemed too young to be driving such a monstrous vehicle, and didn't even appear old enough to have his license. He talked about how many "missions" he had racked up, the term they used for dropping off a load of firefighters or tools and returning to camp. In fire camp we often heard Guardsmen proudly proclaim, "Today I got in my twentieth mission!" like it would earn them the Congressional Medal of Honor. What their desire to complete as many missions as possible meant to us in the back, however, was that we were more often than not at the mercy of a speed-crazed young lunatic who treated their two-and-a-half ton truck with twenty warm bodies in the back as if it were a souped up, off-road 4x4.

Some of the more imaginative Guardsmen took pieces of chalk and wrote confidence-inspiring words on the driver's side door, like, "Greased Lightning!" "Hell on Wheels," "The Devil Makes Do," or my favorite, "Death Before Dishonor!"

We were at the mercy of the military.

Just like everybody else, we joined the other crews heading out, hundreds of firefighters marching in one, long, single file. There was no talking; just crunching, plodding footsteps. Our deuce was waiting.

Getting into a deuce is an art. It's a skill that's hard to come by without a certain degree of practice. The back end of the truck rides a full five feet off the ground — the first and only metal step bar is at least three feet up. When you're carrying a full pack and try-ing to work out the kinks from the day before, three feet is not only inconvenient it's darned near impossi-ble. There weren't any handholds on the back end, either. That would have made it too easy.

Many were the times that someone finally made it to the step bar, only to have their attempt end in an accidental, backward, spread-eagle dive of sorts. In such cases, there was usually a hand of assistance coming from somebody who'd already made it in.

"Here Chris, I'll help you!"

Other times, the person's salvation came in the form of a frantic push from below, motivated by the priceless spirit of self-preservation.

"Grab something, Chris!"

Sometimes, you'd be standing on the road thinking they were in okay — they'd made it into the bed of the truck — only to look up and see a two-hundred pound cursing mass of fire-resistant clothing, leather boots, field pack, and water canteens falling on top of you.

"Look out! It's Chris!"

If we had the time and the common sense, we would take off our packs and hand them up to someone already in the truck. This was much safer, more practical, and was rarely done.

People could board the truck two at a time, one on each side of the rear bumper. With no mishaps, our entire crew could get in and be seated in only a minute or two. The copilot would come around the back, make sure we were seated, shout, "Watch your fingers!" then slam shut and latch the tailgate. It was a really tight fit in the back with a full crew of twenty people packed in, ten to a side facing the other ten. Elbow room was at a premium. We mostly sat with our shoulders crunched together, elbows resting near our belly buttons, gloved hands folded between our knees. We looked like a roughened band of priests awkwardly praying for salvation.

"Everyone got their chin straps on?" the driver always yelled before we started out. It was a new rule that we had to have hard hats secure before we could move out, and it was strictly enforced, ever since the year before, when a deuce in Idaho with a full load of firefighters in the back slid off a logging road and went over the edge, tumbling almost a thousand feet to the bottom of the slope, strewing wreckage and gear all over the hill and killing four of the firefighters. I was on that fire when it happened. Overhead closed the road and we had to take another way in to the fire. I saw some of the survivors later in the day; bloody, bruised, broken. I wish these Guardsmen in California had met them, too. Maybe then they wouldn't have driven so fast. This wasn't a game.

It got to the point where tempers sometimes ran a little high between the firefighters and the Guardsmen/speedsters. One night there was an altercation in the serving line — an entire crew of firefighters pointing their fingers at their camouflage-outfitted driver, shouting bad things at him, the grand finale coming in the form of:

"If you don't drive slower tomorrow, we're going to

tear off your head and spit down your lungs!" In fire camp, that was tender poetry.

We were packed into the back like sheep headed to the auction block. The dull, rumbling drone of fifteen or twenty idling deuces, all lined up and ready to go, drowned out all conversation. When a short, shrill whine punctured the hazy darkness way up ahead, we knew that the lead truck was moving out. Other short, whining bursts would follow in sequence as we followed the leader, one-by-one.

A high whistle and a hard jerk on the gears announced our leaving.

Our truck chugged up the hills, raced straight ahead on the pavement, sped down the steep grades, then churned off onto dirt logging roads. Deuces have the suspension of a brick house. We in the back tended to burp a lot.

The chill wind whirled around us from every direction. It was freezing. With only leather boots and fire pants on my lower half, I tried my best to keep my upper half warm. Even with a tee-shirt, fire shirt, wool shirt, and windbreaker, I really felt the cold. The Nomex heat shield which attached to the back of my hard hat, wrapped around my neck and velcroed shut near my nose kept the wind from blasting down my shirt collar, a minor victory, but still a victory. Other people on the crew would wrap themselves up in heavy-duty emergency blankets, while some would go pretty much "au naturel" with only their standard fire shirt and fire pants to ward off the penetrating cold.

Whatever we wore to stay warm in the back of the truck, paradoxically, also had to be carried in our packs for the rest of the shift. That was the cruel trade-off: freezing during our long drive to and from fire camp, or working like a dog all day under the weight of our packs on the fireline. Some choice. It was crazy. This wasn't something they told me about when I originally signed up to be a firefighter.

Division T

THE TRUCK carrying our tools would be in the same convoy. After we reached our drop point we would often quite literally spill out the back of our rig. We filed past the tool truck, choosing a shovel or pulaski from the open bed, and then gathered around in squads. Our squad boss told us which tool to get.

"Let's see, Jerry, yesterday you were a Shovel. Feel like a Pulaski today?"

"Mary's a mean McLeod. Wanna be the same today?"

Talking was at a minimum; we wanted to save our energy for the hike. Out of habit — practice made perfect — we found our place in line. Jim would say something like, "Let's go," or "We're moving," or "Well, let's get this over with" and then we'd start out.

Walking in a mile or two was the norm. The trail we followed was, more often than not, a fireline that had been completed the day before. Sometimes it took longer to get where they wanted us to start cutting new line. On two occasions, however, the fire had burned so close to Kelsey Fire camp that we merely walked past the dining area, said "See you later" to the food servers, marched down the road for several hundred yards, and began to cut line, starting at the shoulder of the road and working uphill. That was unusual, however, since fire camps are supposed to be located in secure areas, usually a good drive away from the fire itself. Close enough to be handy, but far enough away to be safe.

A hike in was always a good way to warm up and start thinking about the day.

I usually thought of how sore my feet were, and hoped that my leather boots would loosen up when I broke a sweat. They got stiff from the salty perspiration and became supple after walking in them for a mile or so. The salt stains turned the leather of our black work boots bleach-white, especially around the ankles. After a while, it wouldn't even wash away.

When we passed a snag that seemed ready to fall, looming above us, I would think of what a deadly, serious business this was. When I wasn't focusing on trees, I would figure out exactly how much money I had earned the day before, which was quite a trick given the different hourly wages for base pay, hazard pay, nighttime and Sunday differential, overtime, and per diem. If I was especially sharp that morning I would even deduct the taxes, federal and state. Often I thought of how special the other people in the crew had become to me, and how I hoped that I would never let them down. I thought endlessly of how much I wanted to spend time with my family and friends. And I thought how, little-by-little, I was growing to dislike my new life in northern California.

It seemed to me that people did not belong in northern California during this huge burst of fires. Maybe this was nature's way of dealing with all the abuses — development, logging, mining, etc. — that generations had inflicted on her over the years. Nature seemed to be singing a strong, heartfelt message, warning all of us to stay clear. The music was there, but we were all too busy dancing to a different tune, humming the rhyme to ourselves. M-o-n-e-y.

Over time, it started to sink in, however. Nature's melodies began to make sense. Trees fell among our ranks, their outstretched limbs reaching for us, hoping to find us in their embrace. Rocks tumbled effortlessly from above, hissing as they sailed past, missing us by yards but bashing and gouging great pieces off trees not blessed with the gift of mobility. Rattlesnakes, their shelters destroyed, lashed out blindly in angered confusion. Choking dust, blinding smoke, poison ivy and stinging wasps — we had met the enemy, and it was everywhere. Everywhere. And it was us as well, for we were the intruders here. We did not belong. We wore sooty black clothes, as villains should.

Each passing shift took its toll on us. Aging by the day, our faces, smeared with ash and dirt, were etched with new lines and wrinkles. Gut-wrenching smoke coughs, always just a throat-tickle away, became a part of our lives. In restless sleep, we dreamed of fire, and smoke. It was all that we knew. We tried to find peace in our souls, but found only confusion, chaos, and more smoke.

Division U

"YOU WILL have exactly thirty seconds of hot water!" We were getting our pre-shower briefing, courtesy of the National Guard and one of their mobile shower units. The large, dark-green draping tents gave the impression of a M.A.S.H. unit, though ours was far less antiseptic. For this I had waited patiently in line after dinner for almost forty minutes. Men got to shower between 5-6 p.m and 7-8 p.m. Women got dibs from 6-7 p.m. and from 8-9 p.m. I was a little concerned, having had to wait so long in line I might have had to sneak in with the women. I was sure they would have understood. I would have told them that I had a sister, and that would make it all right.

I made it in just in time. The Guardsmen let people

come inside in batches of twelve. That way, there would be four people at each of the three showerhead stands. They rose from the canvas floor like steel hat racks. It smelled like wet smoke inside. There were puddles of soapy water on the floor. One of the fellows in our group wore his tennis shoes — a smart man.

"You will have exactly three minutes to lather up! Use the soap from the trays if you wish!"

"— and if your health insurance is paid up," somebody finished, gesturing with his chin at the grungy bars of community soap. The Guardsman doing the announcing was standing outside so he couldn't hear comments from the gallery.

"You will have exactly one minute of hot water to rinse off! There are paper towels near the exit! Please throw them in the trash when you're done!" Standard fire-camp towels were strong-fiber paper ones about two feet long and a foot wide, unfolded. It took at least half a dozen to get totally dry, but there were almost never enough so we usually had to make do with one or two. If a camouflaged, combat-booted attendant at the entrance gave you just one, then you knew that was all you had coming.

"Are there any questions?"

"Yes, I have a ques —"

"Okay, then here we go!"

Water came gushing forth from the other two showerhead stands, but nothing came out of ours. The seconds were ticking by! No water. Let's Go! C'mon! I hadn't had a shower in four days — what was going wrong!

"Hey, you're standing on the water hose!"

"Oh, jeez, sorry!" New to the modus operandi, the guilty fellow practically leaped off the fire hose-turned shower hose. The hot water began to flow. We'd already lost ten precious seconds, we had to make up for lost time.

The water felt so fresh, so pure, so clean . . . in short, all of the things which we were not. You could not help but purr in pleasure. It felt so good, oh!, how can you describe such pleasure as —

The water went off.

"Okay, that's all! You will now have three minutes to lather up! I suggest you make the most of your time!"

We lathered in frantic silence for a moment, twelve naked men acting as if this might very well be the last shower of their lives. Then, a little dribble of hot water began to trickle out of our showerhead. What was this? It couldn't have been three minutes already! Or, maybe it was that the Guardsman at the switch felt sorry for us and was giving us a freebie! Could he be so generous? What a wonderful human —

"Hey, look at this! I figured out how to get us more water!" The very naked man beside me was jumping up and down in quick little hops on the fire hose, making water come out of the showerhead. It was a miracle! The folks at the other two showerheads simultaneously got wind of the discovery and started hopping. This was great! Free hot water! Let's just see that Guardsman —

"Hey, knock it off in there!" he roared, catching wind of our discovery. "If you do that again you won't get any hot water!" He meant it, too. Everybody stopped hopping. Oh, well, it was nice while it lasted.

The soap was starting to sting my eyes. Three minutes should be just about up. I've never felt more helpless and dependent in my life than to have the final rinsing session in the hands of the Guardsman outside. We knew he didn't like us.

"I'll bet you he only gives us fifty-five seconds," someone cursed.

"Betcha it's only fifty. If we were girls he'd give us *two* minutes!"

"Ready or not, here it comes!" The guy was being a real jerk, but at least he was on time.

Oh, that felt so good! Oh, they should give some kind of award to the person who invented hot water!

The soap had started to dry and it took some scrubbing to get it all off. Holy cow this felt great! The soap was out of my eyes, the first lather went down the drain in a grim lather of soap, grit, grime, soot, and dying bubbles. I hurried to give another quick suds and then a speedy rinse, and pulled the coup off in less than a minute. Oh, I could stand under this hot water for the rest of my —

"Time! Five seconds, four, three, two, one!"

That was all. He'd cut us off.

And it was a darn good thing I took my shower that night, too. The very next afternoon, crews working up and down the canyon heard a tremendous blast that came from fire camp. The hot water tank had mysteriously blown up — rumor had it while the Guardsmen themselves were enjoying a leisurely shower after they stoked it up too high. There would be no more showers for the next several days.

Somebody on another crew shared our feelings. "I hope that one guy didn't get the chance to rinse!"

Division V

AND SO we marched onward, surrounded by the chalky mixture of dust and ash kicked up by our boots. The haze would linger in the air for many minutes, announcing our passage to those crews that followed. Sometimes we would walk through areas completely burned over, where the fireline had not held. It always seemed so sad when that happened. When the line held, it looked like such a miracle; dried grasses, fallen logs and thick stands of beautiful trees, untouched by the blaze, carpeted one side of the line. On the other side of the fireline, lay an endless expanse of blackened ground and charred tree trunks of all sizes.

Crisscrossing the burned area — it went on for as

far as you could see — were scores of long, narrow strips of powdery white ash, all that remained of downed logs after they had burned completely away.

And finally, there were large, slightly sunken areas about the size of a garbage can lid. These were the remnants of ageless stumps which would smolder for days and days as slow-burning embers consumed them an inch at a time, and then spread down into the roots deep underground. These stump holes were our nemesis, particularly at night.

It was all-too easy to accidentally stumble into one of these lurking depressions. One moment you would be walking along, taking a shortcut through the burn or doing a little bit of mop-up — looking up and around for falling trees — and the next moment your leg would unexpectedly plunge into one of these hidden, smoldering cavities. The powdery ash offered no resistance, and in a flash you would find yourself in the trap up to your knee — or worse. Sometimes you could jerk your leg out in time, but usually it would plunge deeper into the glowing embers lurking below. You'd fall down, of course; it's like walking along and suddenly having nothing underneath your lead foot.

Jerking your leg out of the hole was a really good show in itself, especially at night, when stump holes tend to claim the most victims. You'd struggle to get out, but the ground all around was smoking hot. Fiery gravel and burning embers immediately filled your sock, your boot, and the cuff of your pants to over-flow, torching off the hairs on your leg one-by-one. The vigor of pulling free sent showers of embers into the air, swirling and twirling like tiny red fireflies, making little popping and snapping noises as they frolicked in the oxygen.

And so we continued walking. Loose rocks in the trail claimed us as victims, rolling over just after we committed our weight to them, pitching us off balance. The roots that snagged our boots might have laughed at our stupidity, as two or three consecutive people in line stumbled over the same one. Our strides, if you could call them that, reflected our exhaustion. We shuffled doing the Fireline Trudge: put one foot down, shift weight. Watch out for stump holes! Hold onto your shovel. Don't let your pack shift too much. Look out for falling trees! Lift your other foot and place in front of the other. Did you see that rock? Shift weight. Repeat, endlessly.

It's a curious thing, what happens to a firefighter after he or she has been on the fireline for many days. After a week or so of firefighting, the body begins to die. It's true.

Seven days on the line, and the legs just simply refuse to wake up in the morning. Earlier, during the first shift or two, they got tired but it was no big deal. After three days, they were stiff but eventually did loosen up. Days four through day seven were the best of times; legs became strong, adapting to the rigorous schedule.

After those fleeting glory days, however, it was all downhill. Or, rather, from the legs' perspective, it was all uphill. They just didn't respond like they used to, victims of a routine which continuously broke them down and gave them little opportunity for recovery.

Other signs of a decaying body: athlete's foot and jock itch swept through fire camp during the second week, and in these living and working conditions they became unbelievably persistent and painful. We reached the point where we really didn't give two hoots about how we looked, and nobody else did, either. It got worse each day.

On day twelve our crew had just bedded down for the night when out of the smoky darkness we heard somebody shout, "I think I just broke the stink barrier! I can't smell myself anymore!"

Digestive problems began to crop up. In contrast to a normal person, who eats the equivalent of two or three thousand calories a day, the typical working firefighter consumes between eight thousand and *ten thousand* calories each day. Those ham and eggs, sack lunches and hearty dinners with desserts really added up. Dinner might consist of two full steaks, mashed potatoes with gravy (two servings of each), canned corn, three pieces of buttered bread, a fresh lettuce and tomato salad, cottage cheese with sliced peaches, a quart of whole milk, a banana, two candy bars, and a Hostess apple pie, all at one sitting. Strangely enough, during that first week on the fireline — when the body still functioned — after a huge meal like that you still felt hungry, but you knew you'd better not press your luck. You felt great, and fell asleep easily in your bedroll only fifteen minutes after the feast. Your body had reached a new equilibrium.

But then, after a week of this, you began to notice some changes gradually taking place. You don't eat quite as much, and no longer ask for gravy on your seconds of potatoes. That banana just doesn't sound all that great. You only need one slice of bread to soak up the juice from the steaks. You grab the customary Hostess pie out of habit — blueberry, if they had any, which they were usually out of — but don't eat it at the dinner table, saving it for a snack before you brush your teeth. But it doesn't sound too good then, either, so you stuff it into your field pack, and find it there the next day at lunchtime, mashed all over your headlamp.

You continue to work just as hard, but occasionally you feel sluggish and wiped out, with no energy reserves whatsoever. Your body had been a furnace only days before, but the daily stress and strain were taking their toll. You have a problem, but don't yet fully know what it is, or how to deal with it.

More days on the line come and go. That granola bar you munch on the line somehow doesn't settle as easily as it used to. You seem to get easily winded when resuming work after lunch break. At times, dinner loses its appeal, and you eat only one serving, more out of obligation than anything else, thinking, "Dang, I really should eat this to keep my strength up."

On day fourteen, I noticed Jerry putting a roll of candy in his shirt pocket. He offered one to me, but I declined. It had been only five hours since breakfast, and I wasn't hungry. Several minutes later, he came over to where I was taking a quick sip of water. He looked sad, distressed even.

"Man," he said, "you know you've got problems when a Lifesaver makes you belch." Our bodies were falling apart.

And so we worked, cutting new fireline atop a ridgeline, or grubbing out a fire break while ascending

a hill that seemed to go on forever, or scrambling our
way over a creek bottom while chopping out the wil-
lows. Of the three tasks, I disliked the latter one the
most. Slipping and sliding on the wet rocks and moss
— while carrying a sharpened shovel or pulaski — got
really dangerous, especially at night, when our headlamps became our best friends. Creek bottom assign-
ments were especially treacherous because of one
other thing: rolling rocks. If the fire was burning anywhere above, which it usually was on one side or the
other, we had to keep an eye and an ear uphill.

Here's a typical scenario. A good-sized rock, about
the size of a soccer ball, lay nestled high up on a hill,
resting peacefully against the root of a long-dead tree.
It had been there for years and years. A forest fire
burns through the area and ignites the base of the
dead tree. It smolders for hours, even days. The stump
and the roots gradually burn away. Eventually, the
creeping embers finally consume the root that holds
back the rock, and, with nothing to stop it, the rock
tips forward, almost imperceptibly. If a rock could
think, it would shout, "I'm free! Yahoo! Here we go!"

It starts to roll downhill. Gradually, it picks up
speed as it rolls over the soft, unresisting cushion of
ash, kicking up little puffs. Soon, it is happily leaping
its way down the hill, clanging and clicking off stand-

ing rocks. Faster and faster it flies in long, loping arcs, touching down every fifty feet and racing at an incredible speed. It nears the creek, gurgling below, and as its grand finale, hits a charred log, spring-boarding into the air. Still glorying in flight, the tumbling rock plummets into the creek bottom.

Lunch break was nearly over and Alex still wasn't back. At every lunch break, we first had to carve out two little niches for our boot heels and a big one for our behinds. The slopes were so steep that if you did not, you spent half your time slowly sledding downhill and the other half trying to round up your lunch. We never sat one above the other. It was easy to accidentally kick out a rock and have it topple down onto somebody.

Alex showed up just when we were starting to get worried about him. Tall, well-built, sporting a reddish mustache, he wore his hard hat at a rakish angle. Something had happened to him. He was soaking wet, carrying his shovel.

"What happened to you?"

"Rock."

We waited for him to elaborate.

"Big rock." There was a long pause. "Fast rock." It seemed that somehow the big rock, fast rock had made it so Alex could speak with no verbs.

"Are you okay?"

"Okay. Wet."

He slogged his way up the hill and joined us, digging out a place with his shovel. He sat down and opened his sack lunch. We were waiting for him to elaborate. This was going to be good.

"I was panning for gold."

"Panning for gold!"

"Yep."

"With what!"

"With my shovel."

"Your shovel!" (What a great idea!)

"Did you find any gold?"

"Nope. I figured I'd call it quits when the rock almost took my head off."

"Yeah, what happened?"

He chewed thoughtfully on his ham sandwich. "Well, I'd always wondered on these fires if the creeks had any gold in them. I've thought about it for a long time. And now that we're here in California —"

"You felt like being a forty-niner!"

"That's pretty much it. When everybody stopped for lunch, I thought I'd just take a minute and give it a shot. You never know. So I dug up some good-looking gravel from the bottom of the creek and gave it a swirl.

I was perched out there in the middle of the water, standing on some rocks so my boots wouldn't get wet." He humphed at the irony.

"Yeah, so there I was, hunched over my shovel, looking for gold. Everything was really quiet and peaceful, and then **KERWHOOSH!** right in front of me. Never even heard the rock coming. Didn't hear a thing. One second I was looking down at the gravel in my shovel, and the next second, **SPLASH!** I was soaking wet." He took another big bite from his sandwich, making up for lost time.

"I think next time I'll pan with my hard hat. Better than having it on my head!"

Division W

●

ROCK STORIES don't always have a happy ending. Each year, wildland firefighters are seriously injured or killed by rocks that bowl down upon them. Most folks, when they think about forest fires, tend to believe that those who die, or are seriously injured, are victims of the fire itself. But that's not necessarily the case, especially on huge project fires like these in northern California. Fire itself usually claims the most lives when a small fire suddenly turns big. On fires that are already big, it's other things that do the most damage: falling trees, vehicle mishaps, tool accidents, air tanker crashes, and tumbling rocks. Ten firefighters were killed in northern California during the seige, only one of them actually killed by the fire.

Sometimes, way up in a big tree, maybe ten or fifteen feet off the ground, we'd see a big chunk that a high-flying rock had ripped out of the trunk. To see a beachball-sized rock smash into a thicket of trees and shear off a twelve-inch diameter tree is really something. The heavy, ground-shaking thump of a sofa-sized boulder pitching end-over-end is not easily forgotten.

Without a doubt, it's the small rocks that cause the most trouble, though. They make almost no noise at all as they swiftly glide down the hill. Usually there is no warning at all until they smash into a nearby tree or hiss (they really do!) as they rocket past — dangerously close. With small rocks, even if you hear them, their speed and size make them almost impossible to notice amid the backdrop of trees, smoke, and other rocks. And of course, they're impossible to see at night. One fellow on our crew got pegged on the kneecap by a speeding rock the size of a golf ball. His knee swelled to the size of a football. They carried him out on the back of a burro. He was on R and R for several days, and then returned to the crew, still limping.

Warning shouts from others give an indication of a rock's potential for bodily harm. If it's a small rock turned over by the person working ten feet in front of you, uphill, the warning might be a casual, "rock."

A small rock that has rolled twenty or thirty feet will have earned a capital letter.

"Rock."

Fifty feet of linear travel and it gets an exclamation mark.

"Rock!"

Any small, medium or large missile traveling at a good clip gets two hollers.

"Rock! Rock!"

Once a rock has reached terminal velocity it gets its name in headlines.

"ROCK! ROCK!"

If you look uphill and see the tops of some trees waving and swaying — but there isn't a breeze — and then a treetop suddenly plunges down and vanishes, and then another, and another, and the tree-snapping phenomenon is coming downhill straight at you, it's:

"ROCK! BIG ROCK!"

Division X

As we entered our third week on the line, a small note went up on the bulletin board at fire camp, stating that in the first two weeks of the fires in northern California, over 2,000 miles of fireline had been constructed. *2,000 miles!* Another week, another thousand miles.

So we kept working, chopping with our tools and grimacing against the smoke, the hours passing without meaning. We went for days without seeing the sun. The smoke was too thick. It was twilight dark a lot of the time. There were days on end without shadows. No wind blew. It was as if we were in a closed room and smoke was being pumped in.

There was an oxygen tent in fire camp, and sometimes Jerry and I went there after our shift, to breathe pure oxygen from a clear plastic mask. Respiratory infections and smoke inhalation cases were a dime a dozen. People on the line would start coughing so badly they couldn't stop. Their stomachs would go into involuntary contractions, they'd drop down onto their hands and knees, and vomit on the fireline.

It was day twenty-one. We had gone three weeks without hearing the morning call of a songbird, or the sudden tromp-tromp of a deer bounding away through the brush. It seemed that all the wildlife in northern California had packed up and moved away; the only ones stupid enough to remain behind were the firefighters. The only living animal that we had seen was a chipmunk, holding on for dear life halfway up the side of a charred tree trunk. It seemed afraid to move. The poor thing. All of its fur was burned off, and it limped when it tried to scamper away. One of its rear legs did not work. Our only glimpse of wildlife, and it was degraded, disfigured.

Division Y

SAM AND I were cold-trailing a stretch of burned-out stretch of line late one afternoon. Proper cold-trailing involves making absolutely sure that the fire is dead: no smoke, no hot spots, no glowing embers. We were making our way downhill, poking our hands into every gap in the bark, under every log that had somehow made it through the blaze intact. The evergreen forest around us had been turned into thousands of acres of flagpoles: tall, black, barren.

Right in the middle of the trail was a rattlesnake, coiled up tight and very ticked off. It didn't rattle or hiss. It just struck at us without warning, once, twice — three four. Sam and I stepped back out of the way with room to spare. We didn't want to kill it, but other crews were following us. We didn't want somebody to get bitten, so we reached a compromise with the snake. Sam stepped forward and with his shovel casually swept it off the trail. The snake slithered and log-rolled its way out of control down the hill, rattling and striking out at nothing, at everything.

"I feel sorry for rattlesnakes," said Sam.

A few minutes later we got to Kelsey Creek. We picked our way carefully over some loose rocks, coming across a dead, bloated rattlesnake near the water. Someone had killed it with a pulaski and chopped off its rattles as a souvenir. Hopping from rock to rock, we arrived at a flat boulder with a commanding view of a gushing waterfall and a crystal-clear plunge pool. It was beautiful, a small bit of sanity in a world gone totally to hell. We sat down on the boulder and took out some fruit and granola bars.

Sam had been fighting fires for quite a few years; the adventure, the travel, the good money — it was in his blood. He said his even greater love was his family's chile farm in the Rio Grande valley of New Mexico.

"This is the first harvest I've missed in a long time," he said. "My whole family will be out there right now, in the fields, picking chilies."

There was something else he wanted to say.

"You know, I've been doing this firefighting for a long time. If there's one thing I've learned, it's that we have to respect the fire. Fires are living things — they really are. A lot of people don't realize that, but it's true. Just like trees, animals, people — whatever — fires change something into something else. They eat wood and turn it into smoke and heat. Fires breathe, they grow, they reproduce, and they die. Sometimes I even believe fires can think."

Nodding in agreement, I noticed a silvery flash, coming from the water. Sam saw it, too.

"Did you just see something?" he asked.

"Yeah. Did you see what it was?"

"No. Maybe if we keep looking we'll see it." The two of us stared at the water for a moment.

"There!"

"I see it!"

"A fish! Dang, I'd forgotten about fish!"

"Me too! I was expecting to see another snake."

"Look at it!"

The fish jumped clear of the water and threw itself at the waterfall.

"Wow, look! This is great!"

Time after time after time, it jumped out of the water and plunged into the cascading water, only to be driven back into the pool. The fish would slowly circle around the edge of the calm water, biding its time, resting, and then in a flash! it would dart into the current, accelerate, and fly clear of the water, wiggling. It seemed to hang in the air, suspended, diving headfirst into the waterfall, thrashing its tail against the force of the water.

Sam and I cheered. "Go, fish! You can do it!"

Over and over it threw itself into the falls, and it seemed that the water always won. Occasionally, the fish would, for some unknown reason, become badly disoriented. Instead of jumping into the waterfall, it would throw itself onto the rocks at the base of the falls, banging its body and face as it slid down the rocks into the water.

It was time for us to go. We waited for it to make another heroic leap into the waterfall, wanting our memory of it to end on a good one, and then Sam and I bid the fish goodbye with a respectful tip of our hard hats. Life goes on.

Division Z

ANOTHER DAY done. We began our long trudge down the line, stopping to rest several times on the way out. Walking in, in the morning, we did the distance non-stop; heading out in the evening was a different matter altogether. We had been swinging a tool, struggling up ridges, sliding down hills, and watching for falling trees and rocks for the last 13 hours. Several days earlier, we had worked 18 hours, stopping only for lunch. The week before, 96 hours. We were beat. We had our headlamps turned on for the hike back to our deuce. Had to keep an eye out for falling trees and cartwheeling rocks, our faces turned uphill like soldiers passing in review. I don't know why it is, but even if trees look as if they're standing straight — or even leaning slightly uphill — they almost always fall downhill. Those were the ones we were looking out for. Every half hour or so all day one would go, a massive old snag too tired to stand any more.

"BOOM!" They came crashing down and shattered with a noise like a cannon going off. The sound would echo up and down and across the canyon, constant reminders of the dangers we faced. On the other hand, rocks were usually quiet and stealthy. Rocks and trees — they made quite a pair.

Ahead among the trees we saw our deuce.

We filed past the tool truck, tossing our tools into the back without ceremony. Then we took off our packs, got out all our warm clothes, and routinely layered up for our return to fire camp. With sweat-soaked clothes and exhausted bodies, we climbed in and huddled together. Three weeks in northern California and we had seen the end of summer. Trees which somehow survived the blaze gradually changed into their fall foliage over the course of the fire. Some of the trees had even passed their peak, and were shedding leaves.

The truck lurched into gear. It bumped and jostled along, kicking up more dirt than it needed to. The dust swirled around us, mixing with the smoke. After sever-

al minutes, hard hats — chinstraps down, their owners
in exhausted slumber — began to nod forward. A
huge bump and a blast of frigid air across the back of
our necks woke us. Try to go back to sleep. How can
words describe such misery?

We woke again as the truck throttled down, near-
ing fire camp. During the ride, our legs often stiffened
badly; a common sight was to see people step off the
truck's footrest and have their legs collapse. Falling
awkwardly to your knees — or lurching sideways and
pitching headlong — this was always a bad way to
end the day.

There was a Model 20 fire engine near the long
row of deuces where we parked. Somebody on the
engine had chopped down a small spruce tree and
strapped it to the reel of red fire hose up on the back.
There was a cardboard sign taped to the rear of the
pump, with a drawing of Santa Claus.

"Only 99 days until Christmas."

We put on our packs. We lined up and trudged
along the road, made a right turn between the pine
trees — the same right turn our bus had first
made three weeks before — and filed past the command tent.

We walked by the kitchen area. It smelled good. All
right! Pork chops with garlic bread! We waved to the

food servers and then plodded past the generator that rumbled and rocked in its straw bale cradle. Behind the oxygen tent, two guys were sharpening tools with circular sanders that threw off long tails of orange sparks.

It was cold. You could see your breath until it mixed with the smoke. My leather gloves were already starting to stiffen. So were my boots; the salt had leached through and begun to dry and turn white. We found our bedrolls and red packs right where we had left them.

Take off your hard hat. Put on your wool cap. Looks like we'll get to shower on Wednesday. Let's wash our hands and get ready for dinner. Here comes Jim.

"You all ready to eat? Okay, let's line up."

The food servers looked happy to see us. We were glad to see them.

"Those pork chops look good."

"They are. Which one do you want?"

"How about *that* one."

"Okay, here you go. How was your day today?"

"Over."

That night after dinner, Jim came back from his post-dinner briefing with Overhead. He was smiling as

I'd never seen him smile. The way he was walking —
it was as if his feet weren't even touching the ground.
He had the best news of all for us.

"We're going home."

"We're going home?"

"We're going home."

"We're going home! *We're going home!* I can't
believe it, we're going home!"

Our fire was contained and controlled, and we
were going home.

And as I looked up into the night, and saw nothing
but smoke from the other fires still blazing across
northern California — they'd be burning until the first
heavy snowfall — something dawned on me that had
taken three seasons of fire to realize. I'd known it all
along, of course, but deep down I hadn't really understood it.

Whether people try to stop them or not, all fires
eventually go out.

Acknowledgements

Firefighters share intense and at times traumatic experiences on the fireline. Out of respect for the many firefighters I have worked with, the names of certain people, crews, and locations have been changed to help maintain the individuals' privacy.

Firefighting is a team effort, however, and I have been fortunate to work with wonderful folks. The following people in particular need to be recognized for their friendship, loyalty, and assistance: Chris Chiverton, Phil Koepp, Dale and Peggy Rumel, John Mitrovich, Tom Ferrell, Deneyse J. Churchhill, Ken Kerr, Joel R. Stewart, Larry Eppler, Pam Meck, Rick Crawford, John Wiggins, and Ollie Olsen.

A special thanks also goes to the following people or organizations for their part in the book's development: Paula Bailey, Judy Bowlin at The Sherwood Company, Kay Stevens at Thomson-Shore, Inc., S.C.O.R.E., Jeffrey Myers, Russell Dorr, the Albuquerque Public Library, the National Wildfire Coordinating Group (for the use of the pulaski/shovel design), the National Park Service, and the U.S. Forest Service.

Index

Order Information

Additional copies of FIRE READY! may be ordered for $19.95 per book plus shipping. Complete satisfaction guaranteed or your money back.

Call toll free: 1-800-879-4214. Please have your Visa, MasterCard, American Express, or Discover card ready.

For orders by mail: make check payable to "BookCrafters Distribution Center." Please specify that you wish to order FIRE READY!, then mail to:

BookCrafters Distribution Center
615 E. Industrial Drive
Chelsea, MI 48118

Shipping: Please add $3.00 for the first book, and $1.00 for each additional book. All orders will be delivered First Class or UPS to ensure prompt delivery.

Thank you for your order!